Front cover:
Burlington Bay, circa 1850. In this tranquil view Burlington is seen from Appletree Point. The schooner sailing into the harbor is the only indication that Burlington is a bustling port.
By Theodore G. Hopkins, Collection of the Robert Hull Fleming Museum, University of Vermont, gift of Walter Cerf.

Inside front and back covers:
Burlington Harbor, circa 1890. This wonderful photograph shows the excursion steamer *Reindeer* (built 1882), and just to its right a canal schooner.
Courtesy Special Collections, Bailey/Howe Library, University of Vermont.

Quebec City
St. Lawrence River
Richelieu River
& Chambly Canal
Montreal
Plattsburgh
Lake Champlain
Burlington
Essex
Basin Harbor
Whitehall
Lake George
Champlain Canal
Lake Ontario
Oswego Canal
Erie Canal
Waterford
Utica
To Buffalo and Lake Erie
Troy
Albany
Hudson River
Kingston
West Point
New York City

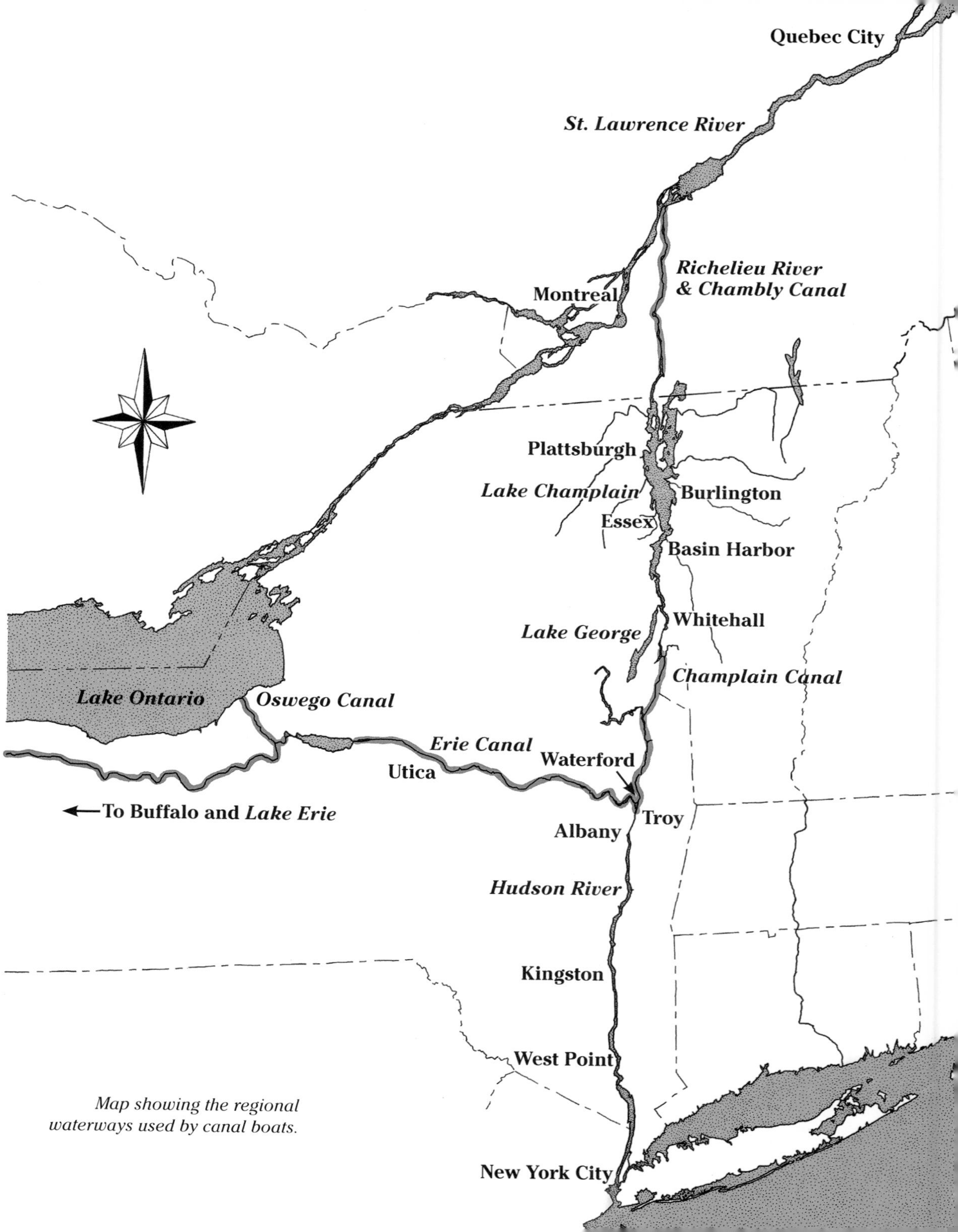

Map showing the regional waterways used by canal boats.

Lake Champlain's Sailing Canal Boats

An Illustrated Journey From Burlington Bay to the Hudson River

Building the Canal Schooner *Lois McClure*

BURLINGTON, VT, 1858.

FROM THE LAKE.

To the Citizens of Burlington, this picture is most respectfully dedicated by the Publisher

H. P. Moore Concord N. H.

Lake Champlain's Sailing Canal Boats

An Illustrated Journey From
Burlington Bay to the Hudson River

to Anne,
I hope this book helps
you get a perspective of
the Museum. I'm looking
forward to working with you.
sincerely
Art
12.15.03

Building the Canal Schooner *Lois McClure*

Arthur B. Cohn

with contributions by

Barbara Bartley, Eloise Beil, David Blow, Lilian Baker Carlisle, Kevin Crisman, Ernie Haas,

Adam Kane, Adam Loven, Alan McKibben, Scott McLaughlin, Roger Taylor & Jane Vincent

Published by the Lake Champlain Maritime Museum

Basin Harbor, Vermont

Publishing History: First edition October 2003
PRINTED IN THE UNITED STATES OF AMERICA

Library of Congress Control Number: 2003111194

Lake Champlain's Sailing Canal Boats/Arthur Cohn
ISBN 0-9641856-3-6 (hardcover)
ISBN 0-9641856-2-8 (paperback)

Designed by Eric A. Bessette, Shadows & Light Design, Burlington, Vermont
Printed by Queen City Printers, Burlington, Vermont

Copy Editors: Susan McKibben, Timothy Etchells, Scott McLaughlin,
Adam Kane, Barbara Benedict, Jennifer Baker, and Joe Ryan

The Lake Champlain Maritime Museum was opened in 1986 to preserve and
share Lake Champlain's extraordinary historical and archaeological legacy.
This special body of information is made available through nautical research,
exhibits, films, school programs, courses, workshops and publications. The
Lake Champlain Maritime Museum is located at beautiful and historic Basin
Harbor in Ferrisburgh with new facilities in Burlington, Vermont.

Frontispiece:
Burlington, Vt. 1858, From the Lake. Perhaps no image
better illustrates the vitality of the Burlington waterfront at
the height of its commercial success. This view overlooking
the breakwater shows an impressive variety of watercraft;
to the right a locomotive is pulling a line of railroad cars.
By H.P. Moore, Concord, New Hampshire, publisher and Endicott
& Co. New York, lithographer, courtesy Shelburne Museum.

ARTHUR B. COHN is the co-founder and
Executive Director of the Lake Champlain Maritime Museum. After a short career in law, he
became a professional diver. He is an adjunct
professor of nautical archaeology at University of
Vermont and the Institute of Nautical Archaeology
at Texas A&M University. He has been the coordi-
nator of the Lake Champlain Underwater
Historic Preserve since its inception in 1985. Art
has served on a U.S. State Department delegation
for the development of a United Nations Treaty for
the Protection of Underwater Cultural Heritage.
His first home was in Nyack-on-the-Hudson and
he now lives in Vermont with his wife Anne and
children Nathan and Genevieve.

*Canal Schooner Sailing off Lewis
Creek in Ferrisburgh, circa 1890.*
The Ray Russell Collection, LCMM.

Sponsor's Foreword

W hen I was young and growing up in Burlington, history was something found only in big, dusty, dull books. We knew we needed to learn it, but all those dates and facts were not very exciting.

With the Lake Champlain Maritime Museum's Burlington Schooner Project, history has come to life! The schooner being built at the foot of historic King Street will be launched in the summer of 2004 and after getting ready she will tour Lake Champlain. In 2005, the schooner will take a Grand Journey through the Champlain Canal and down the Hudson River to New York City. Upon her return to the Burlington waterfront, she will serve our community as a floating classroom and reminder of Burlington's maritime origins and Lake Champlain's commercial era.

The inspiration for the new schooner is a shipwreck that lies at the south end of Burlington breakwater, 40 feet below the surface. Sunk in a violent storm in December of 1876, *General Butler* was discovered by divers in 1980, and this led to the rediscovery of the forgotten sailing canal boats of Lake Champlain. Today, as part of the Lake Champlain Underwater Historic Preserve program, divers can visit *General Butler,* see how it was loaded with cargo and imagine life when canal boats served the lake's bustling waterfront communities.

Today, you can walk along Battery Street and see buildings rooted in Burlington's maritime past. The Stone Store, the Ice House, the Shanty and many others were once part of the waterfront's vibrant commercial activity. A short walk up King Street brings you to the houses of "Admiral" Gideon King and Captains Robert and Andrew White. Unlike *General Butler,* covered with water and invisible to most of us, these buildings survive and continue in use. They have been restored so that we can see how real people lived and worked in this waterfront neighborhood.

In research done for the Burlington Schooner Project all sorts of history has been uncovered—artifacts, tools, boat plans, maps, paintings and photographs, contracts, letters and diaries from real people—and brought to life. So history is found not only in books, but also in attics and storehouses, and sometimes covered with water at the bottom of Lake Champlain.

When I was in school, much of what we are now learning was unknown or overlooked. We were taught the important part Lake Champlain played in the wars for the independence of the United States and, of course, we all appreciated the lake as a wonderful place to swim, skate and sail. But the commercial history of the lake was not yet appreciated.

We now understand much more about how Burlington and many other lake communities emerged along the waterfronts. Mac and I have been delighted to play a part in bringing this history to life. We hope you will enjoy the "living history" in this wonderful book. We encourage you to visit the new schooner and use her to travel back to the time when Burlington Bay was home to dozens of wooden boats and many families derived their living from carrying freight throughout the region. We encourage you to look around your community and join us in the search for hidden history that you can uncover and share with all of us.

Lois McClure
January 14, 2003

Lois and J. Warren (Mac) McClure
Courtesy Mac and Lois McClure.

The Legacies and the Storied Times
of Two Special Waterways

We are delighted to introduce *Lake Champlain's Sailing Canal Boats: An Illustrated Journey from Burlington Bay to the Hudson River*. What a fitting and timely way to showcase the extraordinary cultural history and beauty of the Lake Champlain Basin and the Hudson River Valley.

For centuries, these two waterways played a continuous and central role in often-pivotal events that defined our states, the region, the nation and North America. Generations of native peoples used these waterways for transportation, food and warfare. In 1609, separate English and French expeditions first traveled the lake and river within weeks of each other. Their explorations had profound effects on North America as France, Holland and England became embroiled in a struggle for territorial control that spanned nearly two centuries.

During the American Revolution, Lake Champlain and the Hudson River were highly prized and fought over as key strategic thoroughfares. The Battle of Valcour Island in 1776 on Lake Champlain and the battles of Saratoga in 1777 on the shores of the Hudson River helped give life to the new nation. The sacrifices, political concepts and philosophies born of those times were part of America's founding principles. These historic events and the places where they occurred—West Point, Saratoga, Fort Ticonderoga and Mount Independence—now form a network of historic sites that help define the soul of the nation. Our national rediscovery of these places and their significance has taken on even greater meaning since the tragic events of September 11, 2001.

In the aftermath of the War for Independence, the two waterways anchored their respective valleys as the central arteries of commerce and transportation. Almost anyone moving north or south in these regions traveled on Hudson River sloops or Lake Champlain schooners. In 1807, the transportation world was transformed forever when inventor Robert Fulton proved the utility of steam power on the Hudson River. The very next year, on Burlington Bay, James and John Winans built the world's second successful steamboat. As momentous as the marine application of steam power was, the opening of the Champlain Canal in 1823, for the first time linking the Hudson and Champlain water highways for continuous navigation, had an even greater impact. For the remainder of the nineteenth century, the Champlain Canal and the navigable waterway it created dominated the region's commercial affairs.

The Champlain Canal spawned new industries and fostered prosperity ashore, as well as producing an entire society of maritime laborers. Communities along the lake and river thrived. These days, the passengers and crews on the vessels plying our river, canal and lake more often are there for the magnificent vistas and historic sites than to deliver cargo.

Today, new methods of underwater survey technology are beginning to reveal, as if by magic, the burial places of a vast collection of wooden ships and other structures from our maritime past lying on the bottom of our historic waterways. The states of Vermont and New York are in the forefront of recognizing the value of this public collection and of developing strategies to preserve it.

The illustrated journey captured within these pages connects our past, present and future. The building and launching of the new canal schooner *Lois McClure,* followed by her grand journey from Lake Champlain through the Champlain Canal and Hudson River, will serve as a powerful reminder of days gone by, and it will bring to life for new generations the special and storied history that is shared by the communities along these waterways.

U.S. Senator Patrick Leahy   U.S. Senator Hillary Rodham Clinton
(D-Vermont)   (D-New York)

July 2003

Senators Hillary Rodham Clinton (NY) and Patrick Leahy (VT) 2001. The two senators participated in the 2001 recovery of Revolutionary War artifacts from the site of the Battle of Valcour Island.
Photograph by Eric Bessette, from LCMM Collection.

Burlington, Vermont, circa 1895. Captured in this photograph are the original Burlington
Boathouse (built in 1887 and destroyed by fire in 1901) and the steamer *Vermont II*, perhaps
the most elegant steamer ever to ply the waters of Lake Champlain.
Courtesy Special Collections, Bailey/Howe Library, University of Vermont.

Acknowledgements

Publication of this book and completion of the Burlington Schooner Project would not have been possible without the vision, leadership, and support of Mac and Lois McClure. Their generosity and their desire to provide the public with an insight into the region's maritime commercial history launched this effort.

We are indebted to the Lake Champlain Transportation Company for providing the perfect location to stage the Burlington Schooner Project and to the LCTC staff for providing critical logistical support each step of the way.

Senator Patrick Leahy and his staff and Burlington Mayor Peter Clavelle gave us early encouragement and support for this project and gave us the momentum to move forward.

Vermont Council on the Humanities, a principal promoter of the humanities in Vermont, provided core funding for the Burlington Schooner Project's historical exhibit, which was the basis for this book.

Many fine institutions have provided images for this book; in particular, both Vermont Historical Society and the University of Vermont, Special Collections, Baily/Howe Library have given extensive support in providing illustrations for this work.

Archivist and historian David Blow has made a special contribution to this publication by sharing his decades of research and insights. Lilian Baker Carlisle generously shared her advice, research and editing skills. LCMM Collections Manager Eloise Beil provided her excellent writing and editing skills and LCMM/MRI Project Manager Adam Kane proved his talent and organizational skills in bringing this project to publication.

LCMM staff Jane Vincent and Brenda Hughes provided invaluable support in getting the many details of image selection and administrative support for this project. LCMM archaeologist Scott McLaughlin shared his ground breaking research into the canal era. Mike LaVecchia made valuable contributions to the Burlington Schooner Project section, and Adam Loven provided his drafting skills. Eric Bessette, of Shadows and Light Design, gave painstaking attention to detail and great vision in designing this book. The advice and guidance of Susan and Alan McKibben, of Lake Champlain Publishing, were essential in bringing this publication to completion.

Roger Taylor and Alan McKibben provided their wonderful insights into the Grand Journey of the new canal schooner *Lois McClure.*

My wife Anne, a Burlington girl, generously supported my frequent disappearances from the family to work on this project. My son Nathan and my daughter Genevieve gave their love and patience.

Contents

Steamboat United States, *Schooner* American, *and Canal Schooner* S.H. Witherbee *at Rouses Point, New York, circa 1865*. This extraordinary photograph captures the steamboat *United States*, built in Shelburne, Vermont, in 1847 and condemned after 23 years of service, the schooner *American*, built in Willsboro, New York in 1848 and the canal schooner *S.H. Witherbee* built in Essex, New York, in 1860. From a private collection.

Introduction

The Lake Champlain-Hudson River corridor is one of the most historic waterways in North America. Almost four hundred years ago, in 1609, these routes through the interior of a vast unknown wilderness were "discovered" by European explorers whose names were left behind for posterity. Remarkably, Henry Hudson sailed north on the river later called Hudson in his *Half Moon* almost at the same time that Samuel de Champlain traveled south on the lake he would christen Champlain. Of course these intrepid explorers did not really discover these navigation routes: native peoples had lived around them for millennia. However, Hudson's and Champlain's incursions triggered nearly two centuries of European conflict over control of these strategic waterways for military advantage and control of an immense swath of territory. During the American Revolution, the struggle between the fledgling American Colonies and Great Britain was in large part determined on these inland highways. In 1823, the two waterways were connected by the Champlain Canal, shaping the Lake Champlain region's economic fortunes for the next century.

We have chosen to tell the story from the perspective of Burlington Bay on Lake Champlain, where at the close of the American Revolution, a hamlet formed. That collection of houses grew into the lake's most important nineteenth-century port. Through the window of Burlington's working waterfront we can view the evolution of transportation technology and its influence on society. It is a fascinating story that reflects widely on the region's development; and yet, many people are unaware of the origin of their Lake Champlain and Hudson River communities' maritime roots. As the commercial importance of the lake, the canal, and the river waned in the twentieth century, the communities turned their attention inland.

The rich history of Lake Champlain and the Hudson River is reflected in an invaluable collection of historic artifacts that now resides on their bottomlands. The archaeological sites range from Revolutionary War vessels lost in combat to garbage casually thrown overboard by canal boatmen. Twenty-five years of nautical archaeology on Lake Champlain has revealed that the lake contains one of the nation's best-preserved collections of wooden shipwrecks. Recently, a parallel set of archaeological sites has begun to emerge from surveys of the Hudson River. On Lake Champlain, this growing appreciation for the lake's history and its archaeological collection gave rise to the Lake Champlain Maritime Museum (LCMM) at Basin Harbor, Vermont. LCMM opened in 1986 with a mission to preserve and share this rich history and archaeology with the public. Over the past seventeen years, LCMM has discovered and studied dozens of shipwrecks representing all of the eras of human occupation in the Champlain Valley. The combination of archaeological data from shipwrecks with information from historic records allows a more complete glimpse into the past than either source alone allows.

The study of Lake Champlain's sailing canal boats is a prime example of the dynamic nature of our current understanding of history. The story began to unfold with the 1980 discovery of the wreck of a strange canal boat just off the Burlington Breakwater. The boat had the remains of rigging and a centerboard, as if it were designed to sail, yet it had the shape of a canal boat. Historical research revealed the vessel was *General Butler*, a canal schooner built in 1862 and sunk in 1876 after a dramatic collision with the breakwater. We now know that sailing canal boats were designed to sail on the lake as well as transit the Champlain Canal connecting Lake Champlain to the marketplaces on the Hudson River. Historical research combined with a fortuitous discovery began our journey into uncovering the fascinating tale of Lake Champlain's sailing canal boats. In the years since that first discovery, eleven other sailing canal boats have been located. This book will present the evolving history and archaeology of the sailing canal boat as the story is now known.

These underwater finds were the inspiration for a project to build a replica canal schooner and sail it south from Lake Champlain through the Champlain Canal and the Hudson River to New York City.

Although LCMM has long wanted to undertake the building of a replica canal schooner, it was not until Vermont philanthropists Mac and Lois McClure, who underwrote and endowed the continuing restoration of the Lake Champlain steamboat *Ticonderoga,* put their support behind the idea that it truly came to life. The Burlington Schooner Project is designed to introduce the public to the region's fascinating commercial maritime era. Building a canal schooner also provides a connection to the two canal schooners lying on the lake bottom in Burlington Harbor. *General Butler,* built in Essex, New York, and *O.J. Walker,* built in Burlington serve as the archaeological inspirations.

The new schooner, christened *Lois McClure,* will be launched in the summer of 2004. After launching and fitting out, the schooner will embark upon its Inaugural Tour to historic ports around Lake Champlain. In 2005, the schooner will embark on a Grand Journey through the Champlain Canal-Hudson River corridor, culminating in a visit to South Street Seaport. After her historic journey to New York Harbor, the schooner will return to Burlington Harbor where she will become a tangible reminder to this interconnected regional history and the legacy of Lake Champlain's shipwrecks.

Our understanding of history is not static. New underwater discoveries and historical materials are continuing to come to light and expand our understanding of the working waterfronts once frequented by sailing canal boats. The Lake Champlain Maritime Museum is dedicated to sharing this rich and evolving story and is confident that sharing the unique history of Lake Champlain's sailing canal boats will be both interesting and useful. I hope that the information presented here will encourage new research that will enrich our understanding and knowledge of the canal era.

Arthur B. Cohn
July 2003

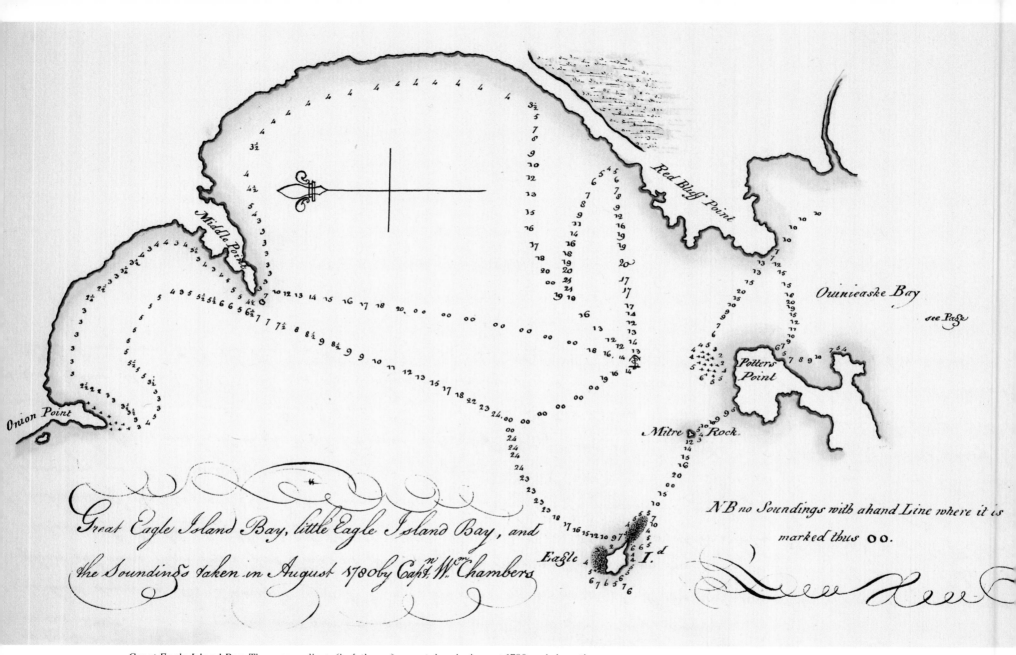

Great Eagle Island Bay, little Eagle Island Bay, and
the Soundings taken in August 1780 by Capt. W.m Chambers

Great Eagle Island Bay. These soundings (in fathoms) were taken in August 1780 and show the
place names then in use for the area now known as Burlington Bay *(Great Eagle Island Bay)*,
Shelburne Point *(Potters Point)*, Rock Dunder *(Mitre Rock)*, Juniper Island *(Eagle Island)*, Lone
Rock Point *(Middle Point)* and Appletree Point *(Onion Point)*.

From Capt. William Chambers, *Atlas of Lake Champlain 1779–1780*, courtesy Vermont Historical Society.

Part I

Before the Canals

Native Settlement ~ 1823

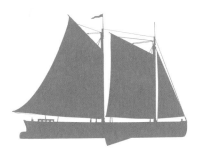

Before the Canals
Native Settlement to 1823

The origins of today's Champlain Valley are rooted in the geological history of North America. The four hundred and eighty million year old fossils located on Isle La Motte and the whale skeleton excavated in 1849 in Charlotte during the building of the railroad provide evidence of the ancient Champlain Sea. The slow moving glaciers were responsible for the lake and mountains we see today.

Human history in the Champlain Valley began more than 10,000 years ago. Native peoples lived here for the entire time and evolved their culture and relationship with the land until they made contact with Western society. This occurred, as far as we know, in July of 1609, when Samuel de Champlain paddled into the "large lake filled with beautiful islands." From his base at Quebec City in New France, Champlain's discovery of the lake ushered in a period of warfare and conflict between Europeans that lasted for the next century and a half.

French and British military forces, each allied with Native Americans fighters, waged war on the frontier settlements of their enemy. This European struggle for control embroiled the Champlain Valley in a chaotic and violent era during which settlement was rare and was located by necessity in proximity to military fortifications. The French extended their range of forts south to the Champlain Valley through the short-lived outpost at Isle La Motte (1666) and the more permanent and impressive Fort St. Frederic (1734). The final act in this European struggle took place between 1755 and 1760 and is remembered as the "French and Indian War." Carillon, Fort Ticonderoga, was built by the French (1755) just when the English had resolved to press their claims. The bloody conflict to control Lake Champlain was essentially won by the British in 1759 when Jeffrey Amherst's army forced the French to retreat from their lake strongholds and return to Canada.

The result of this sequence of events had profound results. For Native American communities the contact with Europeans was a disaster from which they would never fully recover. The fighting devastated their populations and many not killed on the battlefield were lost to new diseases for which they had no immunities. After the fighting stopped in 1760, the Champlain Valley experienced a time of relative stability marked by land speculation and settlement rather than warfare.

The era between 1760 and 1775 saw a few hardy settlers join the few holdovers from the French occupation. Their settlements were few and far between: William Gilliland, in what is now Willsboro, New York; Philip Skene in what is now Whitehall, New York; Peter Ferris, at what is today Arnold's Bay in Panton, Vermont, are a few of the names that survive. The Burlington-Colchester Onion River Intervale, home to native peoples for centuries, now saw the first Europeans trying to establish a foothold at the falls on the Winooski River.

One of the driving forces behind the region's development was the establishment of new townships by Benning Wentworth, the governor of New Hampshire. These towns provided an opportunity for buying and selling land in the Champlain Valley that did not previously exist. Perhaps the most aggressive land speculators were members of the Connecticut-based Allen family. The brothers, Ethan, Ira, Heman, Levi and Zimri, and their kin and neighbors saw in the eastern side of the Champlain Valley the opportunity to get in early and get rich. Ira, the youngest brother, proved to be the most aggressive and his good eye for real estate potential focused the family's Onion River Land Company on Burlington.

Champlain's Battle Scene, July 1609. Samuel de Champlain, explorer of New France, came into the lake with two French soldiers and sixty Algonquin warriors in twenty-four canoes. A skirmish with the Algonquin's enemies, the Iroquois, set the stage for two centuries of near-constant warfare. Champlain's expedition also gave the lake the name it still bears. Drawn by Samuel de Champlain, circa 1613, from *Lake Champlain Tercentenary July 4–10, 1909.*

Lake Champlain, Near Benson, Rutland Co. Vt. This serene image from the southern portion of Lake Champlain, known as the South Lake, shows two Abenaki in the foreground.
Engraved for the Ladies Repository Magazine by R. Hinshelwood, after a painting by D. Johnson, from LCMM Collection.

Rock Dunder, 1909. This massive rock off Shelburne Point at the southern entrance to Burlington Bay is identified by the Abenaki as Odzihozo.
From LCMM Collection.

In a traditional Abenaki legend, the creator of Burlington Bay and the surrounding area, Odzihozo (He Who Shapes Himself), molded himself from the dust of the cosmos. As his hands and arms pushed the earth, the Green Mountains and Adirondacks emerged. When he rose to walk around the land, the impression left by his body formed the lake itself, with one leg on either side of the Champlain Islands. Ultimately, he decided to rest from his labors, and settled down to enjoy this beautiful spot for all eternity. Odzihozo, the massive solitary rock just outside Burlington Harbor, remains sacred to the Abenaki. They still honor him with offerings of tobacco.

In the centuries before European colonization of North America, native people in the Champlain Valley often established villages at locations where rivers flowed into the lake. One such settlement was located near the mouth of the Winooski (the Onion River). Native people of the valley formed relationships with French fur traders and missionaries in the seventeenth century. This Abenaki-French alliance kept most British settlers from moving into the lands later known as Vermont until the end of the French and Indian War in 1760.

⊰⊱

❧ *The Onion River Land Company and the Settlement of Vermont* ❧

Winooski River, circa 1900. The first pre-Revolutionary War settlement in the Burlington area was at the falls on the Winooski River.
From LCMM Collection.

By 1760 settlers and speculators of the British colonies of Connecticut and Massachusetts began to look northward for open land. Brothers Ethan and Ira Allen of Connecticut were attracted to the wilderness areas east of Lake Champlain. While Ethan Allen is famous for his role in the Revolutionary War, Ira laid the groundwork for the city of Burlington. In 1773, Ira Allen conducted the first formal survey of the area, mapping territory from the mouth of the Winooski River to the Green Mountains. He later recalled that he had been charged "to look out for the best place for trade, at or near Lake Champlain…which I faithfully attended to, and gave Burlington Bay the preference of any part of the country." Confident that "Burlington would, from its situation, become a place of consequence… I went and pitched a number of hundred acre lots contiguous to Burlington Bay."

Shortly afterward, Ira, Ethan, Heman, and Zimri Allen, and their cousin, Remember Baker, banded together to form the Onion River Land Company, and received title to substantial quantities of land grants issued by New Hampshire. They settled on the Winooski, building first at the falls to take advantage of the source of waterpower and its sheltered location. The town took its name, perhaps by mistake, from the charter granted by New Hampshire in 1763 to Edward Burling, who owned land in Colchester.

In 1764 the British placed this same territory under the authority of the colony of New York. Soon, settlers with competing land claims resorted to force to assert their titles. In the early 1770s, Ethan Allen helped to form a militia known as the "Green Mountain Boys" to discourage New York settlers and land agents.

Cover of Ethan Allen's Anti-Yorker publication, 1781. This presented the Vermonter's point of view on the controversy between rival landowners holding title from two different governors.
From a private collection.

Ira Allen (1751–1814). "Five sevenths of the Town of Burlington belonged at different times to Ira Allen," *Vermont Historical Gazetteer,* 1867.
Courtesy Special Collections, Bailey/Howe Library, University of Vermont.

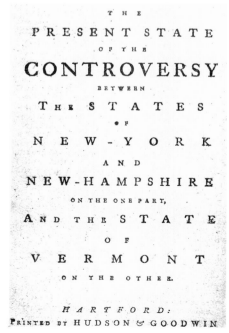

THE

PRESENT STATE

OF THE

CONTROVERSY

BETWEEN

THE STATES

OF

NEW-YORK

AND

NEW-HAMPSHIRE

ON THE ONE PART,

AND THE STATE

OF

VERMONT

ON THE OTHER.

HARTFORD:

PRINTED BY HUDSON & GOODWIN

Ethan Allen at the Taking of Fort Ticonderoga, May 10, 1775.
Ethan Allen demanded the surrender of the fort, "In the name of the Great Jehovah and the Continental Congress."
Courtesy Library of Congress.

God Bless Our Armes. This ink and watercolor shows the American squadron under the command of General Benedict Arnold. Although Burlington saw no action, settlements at Winooski and Shelburne were abandoned during the war. New research suggests the cutter *Lee* may have been abandoned in the Winooski River during the aftermath of the October 11, 1776, naval engagement at Valcour Island.

By Charles Randle 1777, courtesy Fort Ticonderoga Museum.

By the 1770s the American colonists were increasingly dissatisfied with British authority. The Boston Massacre occurred in 1770; the Boston Tea Party followed in 1774. On April 18, 1775, British troops fired into groups of citizens assembled at Lexington and Concord, and Paul Revere saddled his horse and took off on his famous ride to call the rebel colonists to arms. Less than a month later, on May 11, Ethan Allen, and his Green Mountain Boys, joined forces with Benedict Arnold and seized Fort Ticonderoga from the unsuspecting British.

The ever-present threat of military activity on Lake Champlain disrupted most efforts at settlement and trade during the war years, from 1775 through 1783. Military activity on the lake focused on strategic points such as St. John's (St. Jean) at the northern end and Fort Ticonderoga and Mt. Independence further south where the lake narrows. The Burlington area saw action only once, when the Americans abandoned the cutter *Lee* in the Winooski River after the Battle of Valcour Island. As soon as the war ended, settlement of the area resumed. Families returned to the Onion River Falls and to Colchester Point, and established the first permanent settlements at Burlington Bay.

Top: *A View of the New England Arm'd Vessels at Valcour Bay on Lake Champlain—11 October 1776*. The vessels from left to right: *Revenge, Washington, Philadelphia, Congress, Spitfire, Lee, Royal Savage* (foreground), *Boston* (in the background between the topsails of the *Royal Savage*), *Jersey* (partly hidden behind the peak of the *Royal Savage's* mainsail), *New Haven, Providence, Connecticut, New York, Enterprise,* and *Trumbull.*

By Charles Randle, 1777, courtesy National Archives of Canada.

Bottom: *A View of His Majesty's Arm'd Vessels on Lake Champlain—11 October 1776*. The vessels are shown sailing south before the battle. They are from left to right: *Carleton, Inflexible,* a cutter-rigged gunboat, *Maria, Loyal Convert, Thunderer;* and several small British gunboats in the background.

By Charles Randle, 1777, courtesy National Archives of Canada.

In the years following the American Revolution, returning homesteaders and new settlers flocked to Vermont, lured by the dream of acquiring land. When the Republic of Vermont joined the United States in 1791, the population of Vermont stood at 85,341. Twenty years later, the population had increased to 218,000, with more than half under 16 years of age. Burlington, Guilford, Windsor and Middlebury competed for the distinction of being the largest town in the state. Burlington's location gave the community a competitive edge, and the waterfront bustled with ship building and commercial enterprises.

Burlington grew and prospered as local merchants established connections with merchants in distant ports. Ethan and Ira Allen traded with Canada through their Loyalist brother Levi, who had settled there after the war. John Jacob Astor, of New York, made a fortune in furs. His Burlington agent, Gideon King, Jr., who, for the first quarter of the 19th century, eventually controlled nearly half of the commercial vessels on Lake Champlain, arrived in Burlington in 1788 with his father, Gideon King, Sr., and four brothers. The senior Gideon King built a tavern and embarked on commercial enterprises. Gideon, Jr., 14 years old when the family arrived in Burlington, two years later started in the lake shipping business. In the years between 1790 and 1814, at least 30 commercial sailing vessels of 30 tons or more were built in Burlington, Vermont, and in Whitehall and Essex, New York. In one way or another, King controlled most of these ships: either he advanced money to build them, or he purchased them outright. His involvement earned him the nickname "The Admiral of Lake Champlain." King remained the dominant figure in lake commerce until his death in 1826.

"Admiral" King Builds a Fleet

About 1790, [Gideon King and Job Boynton] went to Canada, found some old War vessels, and fitted up two schooners, which they sailed between Burlington and St. John's. These were heavy and unmanageable affairs and at the present day [1867] would be considered as entirely useless. King's was called the "Horse Boat" because he had a place in it arranged especially for carrying horses to and from St. John's…There were no rats here until they were brought from St. John's, in the old Horse Boat, by Gideon King.

—*Vermont Historical Gazetteer*, 1867

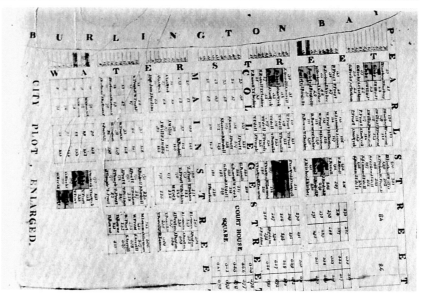

Map of Burlington, Vermont, 1798 (detail). This early map of Burlington shows the small, long, and narrow water lots. This land division provided maximum opportunity for access to the all-important waterfront. Also note the lack of wharf and dock facilities at this early date.

By William Coit, courtesy Special Collections, Bailey/Howe Library, University of Vermont.

View of Whitehall, New York, circa 1820. This view of Whitehall, which predates the opening of the Champlain Canal, shows several sloops and schooners along the waterfront. This is one of the best images of Lake Champlain's early commercial vessels. Plate No. 21, by Jacque Milbert, from LCMM Collection.

The lake's international boundary forced traders to contend with the constantly changing regulations issued by the governments of the United States, Canada, and Britain. Official policies at various times endorsed free trade, no trade, or various restrictive licenses, but settlers and merchants somehow continued to transact business across the border. American timber, potash, pearl ash, furs, horses, cattle, sheep, fish, cheese, grain, maple sugar, flax, and tobacco arrived at Canadian markets where they were exchanged for salt, rum, gin, and luxuries like tea, coffee, chocolate, textiles, and other manufactured goods imported from Europe. Ships and smaller watercraft, as well as log rafts loaded with goods, made the trip when the lake was open; when it froze, goods from as far away as Boston were hauled to Canada by horse-drawn sleighs.

> *[Daniel] Wilcox being the first boat builder upon the Lake, adopted the style of vessel built at New London, which accounts for the superior models of the sloops here, which it will be observed are not like the heavy Dutch sloop of those days, in use upon the Hudson, but like the clipper vessels which were built at New Haven and Hartford...before the days of the steamboats.*
> —*Vermont Historical Gazetteer,* 1867

> *There were not over seven framed houses in the whole village at the time, the forest being almost unbroken, except on Water Street...*
> —Observations by Britain's Prince Edward during a visit to Burlington, February 1793. *Vermont Historical Gazetteer,* 1867

Burlington in 1800

Population: 815
Town Size: 71st in State
Population under age 26: 70%
Village of Burlington Bay contains: 6 innkeepers, 5 retail merchants, 5 lawyers, 1 silversmith, 2 shipwrights, 1 blacksmith, 1 cabinetmaker, 2 coopers, 1 physician, and 1 chairmaker.

The *Vermont Centinel,* a weekly newspaper, began publication in Burlington in 1801. Within six months, the newspaper had a circulation of 800. News was slow to reach Burlington. New York news took about two weeks, while news from London and other European capitals took about twelve weeks.

The Vermont I *Fitting Out in Burlington Bay.* The city of Burlington grew out from the corners of King and Water (now Battery) streets. The city's early shipbuilding took place at this location, and it was here, under a large oak tree, that the world's second successful steamboat, the *Vermont,* was built and launched in 1808.

By Ernie Haas, 2001, courtesy of the artist.

VERMONT CENTINEL.

Vol. IX.   BURLINGTON, *Friday,* June 30, 1809.   N 14.

VERMONT
STEAM BOAT.

THE Vermont Steam Boat has been built and fitted up, at great expence, for the convenient accommodation of Ladies and gentlemen who wish to pass Lake Champlain, with safety and dispatch. She will make the passage of the Lake, 150 miles, in the short time of 24 hours; and her arrival and departure has been so arranged as to meet the Southern Stage at White Hall, and complete the line to St. Johns, L. C. The Steam Boat will sail from St. Johns every Saturday morning, exactly at 9 o'clock; will pass Cumberland Head about 5 o'clock on the same day, and arrive at Burlington at 8 o'clock in the evening. Leave Burlington at 9 the same evening and arrive at White Hall, at 9 next morning. Returning, leave White Hall every Wednesday at 9, A. M

Vermont Steamboat. 1809 newspaper article from the *Vermont Centinel,* Burlington, Vermont.
From Ross, *Steamboats of Lake Champlain.*

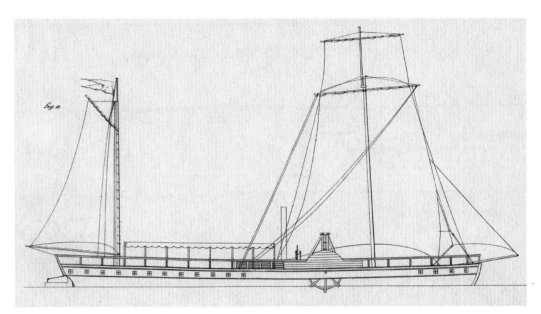

Fulton's Paragon. Built in 1811 for use on the Hudson River between New York and Albany.
From Marestier, *Memoir on Steamboats.*

Because transportation was central to economic trade, inventors in Europe and America searched unceasingly for faster and more reliable boats and ships. In 1807, Robert Fulton launched the world's first successful steamboat on the Hudson River. The next year John and James Winans started construction on their steamboat at the Burlington waterfront under a large oak tree not far from the site of the present Champlain Transportation Company. The hull of the steamboat *Vermont* was launched in the summer of 1808; the completed boat entered service in June, 1809, as the second steamboat in the world. While sail-powered watercraft continued to operate, steamboats captured the popular imagination and, because of their economic advantage, dominated the world's waterways for the next century.

⁍ *Embargo, Smuggling and the* Black Snake *Affair* ⁌

Even as the first American steamboats opened an era of fast, reliable transportation, international events created new barriers to American trade, which was especially burdensome for residents of the Champlain Valley. The British, battling Napoleon Bonaparte, needed to man their navy adequately. Volunteers were no longer available so they resorted to kidnapping, or "impressing" merchant sailors. The British searched American vessels for deserters, and often pressed American sailors into service as well. Parliament refused to address the growing list of American grievances, so in 1807, President Thomas Jefferson ordered all British ships out of American waters, and enacted a total embargo on American trade with Britain and her colonies, including Canada.

British merchants soon found other outlets for their goods, but the embargo devastated American trade. For inhabitants of the Champlain Valley, Canadian ports provided the only viable outlet for local products, and trade relationships were well established. Smuggling became widespread as Champlain Valley residents devised ways to evade restrictions. Harried customs officials found it nearly impossible to enforce the embargo, even with militia support, and government officials seemed reluctant to use force against private citizens.

⁘

Log Raft on Lake Champlain. In the decades that followed the Revolutionary War, harvesting and rafting Champlain Valley timber was a thriving enterprise. By the middle of the nineteenth century, little was left of the old growth forest.
From LCMM Collection.

…as Congress, under the pretense of saving our commerce from depredations, have totally destroyed it…

—*Vermont Centinel*, February 1809

The most notorious local confrontation between smugglers and U.S. Customs officials took place on the Winooski River in August of 1808. The customs service learned that the smuggling vessel *Black Snake* would be transporting a cargo of potash to Canada. They sent the twelve-oared revenue cutter, *Fly,* to intercept the smugglers. The clash left two soldiers and the captain of *Fly* dead, and another officer seriously wounded. The smugglers were captured and brought to trial, and Cyrus B. Dean, a member of the crew, was sentenced to death. Some 10,000 people gathered in Burlington to witness the hanging. Three other men from *Black Snake* brought to trial were convicted; two were sentenced to fifty lashes and ten years imprisonment, the third to imprisonment only. Although the captain of the vessel, Truman Mudgett of Highgate, Vermont, was tried, the jury could not reach a verdict and the case was finally dismissed.

To The People of Vermont. This broadside was produced in 1808 after the *Black Snake* Affair.
Courtesy Vermont Historical Society.

TO THE PEOPLE OF VERMONT.

FELLOW CITIZENS,

IT IS DONE ! The cup of guilt is full ! Treason, rebellion and murder stalk abroad at noon-day ! Our land has been stained with the blood of our citizens, acting in defence of the government and laws of our country. By whom ? A foreign foe ? No : but, (horrid to relate !) by the bloody hands of domestic traitors.

Capt. JONATHAN ORMSBY, a respectable farmer, belonging to Burlington ; Mr. ELLIS DRAKE and Mr. ASA MARSH, two respectable young men, belonging to Capt. Pratt's company of militia, stationed at Windmill Point, were all killed at Burlington, on Wednesday the 3d instant, about noon, in a most wanton and barbarous manner, by a party of insurgents, employed in smuggling potash into Canada, in violation of the laws. The Collector detached Lieut. Farrington, a sergeant and twelve men, in pursuit of a boat, which had gone up Onion river after a load of potash.—The Lieutenant found the boat and took possession of her, notwithstanding the insurgents threatened to blow out his brains if he attempted to meddle with her. The Lieutenant dropped down the river, with the cutter and the boat he had taken, about half a mile ; when the insurgents fired upon him and killed Drake. The Lieutenant then ordered both boats to be rowed on shore, near the place whence the fire proceeded : he landed with his men, and ascended the bank of the river ;—immediately the insurgents discharged a large gun, called a wall-piece, the barrel of which is eight feet in length, and was loaded with sixteen ounce balls, and some buck shot—which carried instant death to Captain Ormsby and Mr. Marsh, severely wounded the Lieutenant in the head, the left arm, and slightly wounded him in the right shoulder. Capt. Ormsby had been laboring in his field during the forenoon, near the fatal spot, was on his return to dinner, had just reached the place where the government troops entered the road, when the murderous discharge took place, which, at the same instant, sent two souls companions into eternity.

If any thing can add to the horror of this, too horrid scene, it is the observation of certain federal characters of the vicinity, who even lay claim to the name of high respectability, tending to screen the assassins, and throw the whole weight of guilt on the part of the government.——Says one, *The men were sent here by Penniman to steal an empty boat, and died like fools*—Says another, *I hope to God Penniman will be hung for it*—Says another, *I should care but little about it, if I did not fear it would influence the ensuing election*—Says another, on hearing of the melancholy event, *I am glad of it, they are republicans who are killed.*——Such was the current of expression which poured from the mouths of federalism, while the blood was still gushing from the weltering bodies of our countrymen, murdered by federal hands at mid-day, within the boundaries of that town which boasts itself of being the strong hold of federalism, and some of whose principal merchants furnished the insurgents with powder and ball, for the express purpose of performing this bloody work.

The federalists now begin to lengthen their faces, and pretend to feel regret for the transaction ; but their hypocritical tears will not avail them. This horrid deed has been done by their procurement ; they are partners in the guilt of the perpetrators, and they are accountable to their country and their God, for all the blood that has been shed.

When a large body of men, and more especially those in the higher walks of life, who arrogate to themselves all the virtue, all the talents, and all the religion of the country, combine together for the purpose of opposing the laws of their country ; when they openly and publicly, by printing and speaking, treat the government and the officers of the government, from the President of the United States down to the lowest executive officer, with abuse, ridicule and contempt ; when they trample on the laws of their country, by daily exciting, both by precept and example, the violation of those laws by force and arms ; when they exult at the success of the insurgents in every act of treason they commit ; when they

bid defiance to government, and threaten the officers with assassination if they attempt to do their duty ; when with more than savage barbarity they exult over the bleeding bodies of our murdered citizens ; and when they even insult the faithful soldier while oppressed with grief at the loss of his beloved comrades :—then is the cup of guilt full ; then is it time TO ROUSE IN DEFENCE OF YOUR COUNTRY AND YOUR LIVES.

This is no ordinary contest. It is not a simple question, who shall be governor and councillors ; but it is a struggle for the existence of your government ; for the protection of those rights purchased with the blood of your fathers ; and for the protection of your lives. Should that faction whose hands are still reeking with the blood of your brethren, come into power, what have you to expect ? If they have done these things in the face of law, in the face of authority, what will they do when clothed with power ? This bloody scene is but an opening wedge to the measures they would pursue. The tragedy of Robespierre would be reacted in the United States ; and every distinguished character, who is a friend to his country, might expect to be sacrificed to the malice of an unprincipled and vindictive faction.

Fellow citizens, on you depends the fate of your country—by your suffrages at the approaching election, you will decide, whether you deserve the name of freemen ; whether you are worthy of your fathers ; whether you will defend the government of your country, and protect your wives, your children, and your own lives ; or whether you will tamely give up your dear bought rights, and submit your necks to the axe of the guilotine.

By supporting our present patriotic governor and councillors, you will perpetuate the existence of our government, and transmit to posterity the blessings we now enjoy.

By neglecting to attend the poll, or by voting for the federal ticket, you will entail on your country all the horrors of slavery, oppression and murder.

MONITOR.

FROM BURLINGTON BAY ON LAKE CHAMPLAIN.

From Burlington Bay on Lake Champlain. In this circa 1811 view, six sloops make their way to and from the harbor between (left to right) Shelburne Point, Rock Dunder, and Juniper Island.
From a private collection.

20

⫷ *The War of 1812* ⫸

As the nation entered the War of 1812, Lake Champlain was again a contested frontier. Military units were assembled in Burlington and Plattsburgh to prevent British forces from taking control of the waterway. This action crippled lawful traffic on the lake, but smuggled goods still flowed from the Champlain Valley and helped support the British effort.

By the fall of 1812, the site known today as Battery Park was an army camp for more than 4,000 regulars, while the civilian population of Burlington (as of 1810) numbered 1,690. Cannons were put into place "to defend the town and to protect the steamboat *Vermont* and numerous watercraft that took shelter beneath the guns."

Throughout 1813, tension remained high. On one occasion, British vessels sailed close to Burlington's shore, and fired on the bluff. Some families sent women and children to the relative safety of outlying towns. "Admiral" King, however, continued to prosper. His vessels transported troops, provisions and stores for the government, and he took the opportunity to load merchandise for the local community on the return trips.

Matters came to a head on September 11, 1814, with the Battle of Plattsburgh Bay. The guns could be heard at Burlington and spectators in the tower of the University of Vermont building witnessed battle smoke. Every available boat was requisitioned to take volunteers across to the opposite shore.

⫷⫸

The Battle of Plattsburgh Bay. This watercolor captures the conflict between American and British naval and land forces on September 11, 1814. The American victory at Plattsburgh led to a secure lake and the eventual conclusion of the wider war. From a private collection.

An eyewitness account describes the battle: "*…by 8 o'clock on Sunday morning… the wharves were completely naked of watercraft, and Burlington was almost a 'deserted village.' The sound of artillery had been heard at short intervals from sunrise… but about half past nine the cannonading became incessant, and it was now rendered certain that the fleets were engaged… if the enemy proved successful his ships would soon be pouring broadsides into the town… At length, about 9 o'clock in the evening, a person who had viewed the naval engagement from Grand Isle, opposite Cumberland Head, came in with the cheering intelligence that the naval victory was ours and that the British land force had precipitately fled. The news was eagerly spread, and the Sabbath stillness was broken by hearty cheering on all sides. Tar barrels were procured and bonfires assisted to proclaim the general rejoicing.*"

—Reminiscences of a Retired Printer, *Burlington Free Press and Times,* 1890

⊰ *The Phoenix Tragedy* ⊱

After the War of 1812, Champlain Valley residents were eager to get back to business. The steamboat *Phoenix,* built at Vergennes by the Lake Champlain Steam-Boat Company, commenced operations in 1815, and the steamboat *Champlain* was launched in 1816. For the next two years, these steamboats made regularly scheduled north-south runs on the lake, linking Burlington to Whitehall, New York, and St. John's (St. Jean), Canada.

Phoenix departed from Burlington as usual on September 4, 1819, but shortly after midnight, she caught on fire. Flames enveloped the center of the vessel, and passengers raced for the lifeboats. Unfortunately, someone had cut the second lifeboat loose prematurely, and eleven people were left on board. Although five survived by holding onto wooden planks and furniture, six perished. Burlington residents saw the light of the burning steamer, and sloops loaded with supplies sailed out to rescue the survivors the next morning.

Some people were not enthusiastic about steamboats. They feared malfunctions would lead to explosions or fire, and established sailing interests certainly viewed steamboats as unwelcome competition. The first newspaper account of the disaster declared, "The fire was occasioned by a candle or candles, left in the pantry, and not from the machinery." The Lake Champlain Maritime Museum's recent investigations suggest that the fire may have been the result of sabotage by competing sailing interests. If the intention was to dampen public enthusiasm for steamboat travel, the plot failed. By 1832, eight additional steamboats had been launched on the lake, with more to follow.

⊰⊱

Lake Champlain Steam Boat. A September 30, 1815, newspaper announcement of the beginning of service for the recently completed *Phoenix.*
Courtesy Special Collections, Bailey/Howe Library, University of Vermont.

Phoenix *Burning, 1819.* On the night of September 4, 1819, while en route from Burlington to Plattsburgh, the steamboat *Phoenix* caught fire. The vessel was destroyed and six people lost their lives.
A modern conjectural painting by Ernie Haas, from LCMM Collection.

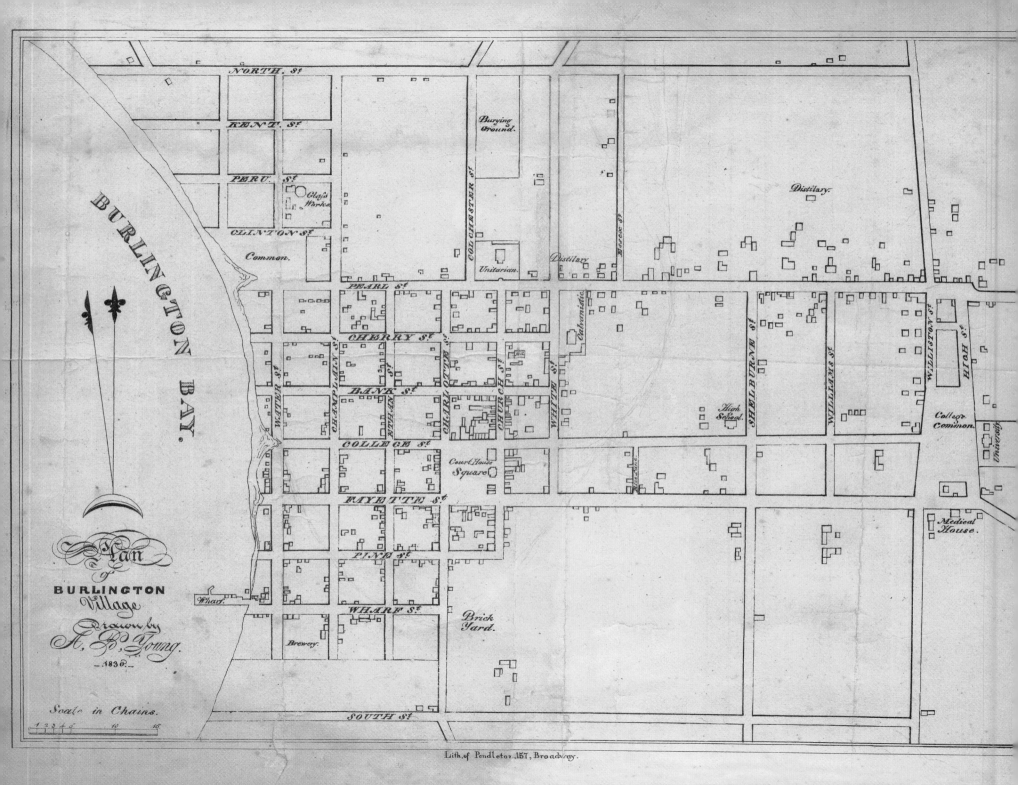

BURLINGTON BAY.

NORTH. St

KENT. St

PERU. St

Glass Works

CLINTON St

Common.

Burying Ground.

COLCHESTER St

Distilary.

Distilary.

Unitarian.

PEARL St

CHERRY St

WATER St

CHAMPLAIN St

PINE St

CHARLOTTE St

CHURCH St

WHITE St

Calvanistic.

Calvanistic.

High School.

COLLEGE St

BANK St

St. PAULS

WILLISTON St

HIGH St

UNIVERSITY

College Common.

COLLEGE St

Court House Square

FAYETTE St

PINE St

Medical House.

Wharf.

Brewery.

WHARF St

Brick Yard.

SOUTH St

Plan
of
BURLINGTON
Village
Drawn by
A. B. Young.
1830.

Scale in Chains.
1 2 3 4 5   10   15

Lith. of Pendleton 157, Broadway.

Part II

The Boom Years

1823 ~ 1900

Map of Burlington, 1830. This extraordinary map by Ammi Young shows the outline of every building in Burlington at that time. The University of Vermont Historic Preservation Program has recently utilized the map to create an inventory of pre-1830 structures still standing.
Courtesy Special Collections, Bailey/Howe Library, University of Vermont.

The Boom Years and the
Sailing Canal Boats of Lake Champlain
1823 ~ 1900

As the community of Burlington emerged along the crescent-shaped beach, the foundation was being set for even more dynamic growth ahead. Shipbuilding activities and clever merchants were giving Burlington a central place in the next phase of growth. Its large and commodious bay and its connection to the vast region to the east made Burlington Bay a natural marketplace. The evolution of steamboats made for more predictable travel and helped tie Burlington into the network of emerging lake ports all along the lake's length and beyond. But the most momentous change was just on the horizon.

The first effort to connect Lake Champlain and the Hudson River via canal began in 1792, but ended shortly afterwards in failure. In the wake of the Inland Lock Navigation Company's demise, a new effort was launched by New York State in 1817. With little tangible assistance from Vermont, New York interests authorized and invested in the sixty-three mile link of these two natural water highways. In 1823 the Northern Canal was completed and although its opening was expected to facilitate commerce, the new canal exceeded even its most ardent supporters' expectations.

The Champlain Canal ushered in the boom years. The water connection to markets along the Hudson River opened up new opportunities. Before, getting heavy products like iron ore or stone to the marketplace economically had not been possible. The opening of the canal triggered a geometric increase in annual tonnage moved upon the river and lake. To accommodate this increase, new docks and wharves were built on Burlington Bay, and in 1826 the first federally-funded lighthouse was established on Juniper Island. This was followed in 1837 with the first phase of the Burlington Breakwater's construction, designed to protect shipping in Burlington's spacious but exposed harbor.

In 1980, when two young divers, Scott MacDonald and Dean Russell, discovered *General Butler* laying intact on the west side of the Burlington Breakwater, they triggered an archaeological study that led to the rediscovery of the Lake Champlain sailing canal boat. During the next decade of research, like a mystery's clues being discovered by a detective, the story of the Lake Champlain sailing canal boat began to unfold. Each new reference helped bring into better focus the origin and use of these once common freight carriers. It is now known they appeared on Lake Champlain in 1823, simultaneous with the opening of the new Champlain Canal. While never as numerous as their cousins, the standard towed canal boat, the sailing canal boats developed their own niche of operations that gave them increasing viability until changing times and new, more efficient transportation systems doomed them to extinction. They now exist as a handful of archaeological sites on the lake bottom and in the emerging historical record presented here.

The evolution of transportation technology continued the trend. At the end of 1849, the first railroads reached Burlington Bay and connected the village with established and new marketplaces. It also afforded a more stable base of year-round transportation and it was Burlington's connection to water and rail that really sparked the next phase of economic growth. The completion of the Chambly Canal in 1843 provided an all water route from Lake Champlain to the St. Lawrence River. Fortunately for Burlington, the Champlain Valley could import timber from the Canadian forests using this new route. During the first half of the nineteenth century, land clearing, log rafting, potash manufacturing, charcoal production, as well as lumbering had cleared the Champlain Valley of every tree worth cutting. Economic famine loomed in the distance.

The Chambly Canal, built to revive once active Champlain Valley trade with Canada, had an opposite effect. Instead of products of the Champlain Valley moving north, boatloads of Canadian lumber traveled south. The importation of Canadian lumber to be processed and piled in the yards of Burlington, then transshipped by water and rail to New England markets, created the backbone of commerce for the remainder of the nineteenth century. A tariff passed by Congress designed to protect American lumber interests in the West put an end to the Burlington lumber business. The close of the century saw the ending of one era and the beginning of the next.

The Opening of the Champlain Canal, 1823

View of the Junction of the Northern and Western Canals at Waterford, New York, circa 1825.
From a private collection.

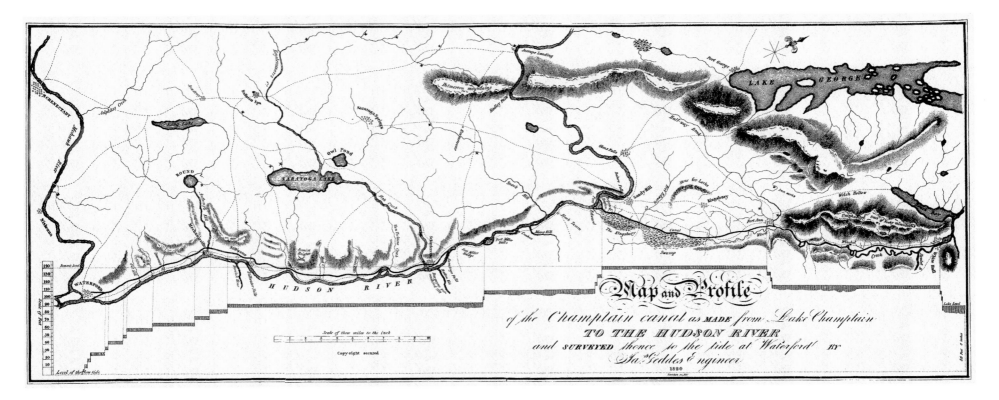

Map and Profile of the Champlain Canal, 1820. This map laid out the route and displayed the elevations of the new Northern or Champlain Canal, which connected the waters of Lake Champlain to the Hudson River. From a private collection.

The opening of the Champlain Canal in 1823 was possibly even more important than the advent of steamboats in defining nineteenth-century trade on Lake Champlain. The canal completely changed the economic focus of the Champlain Valley. Early on, the major commercial traffic flowed north through the Richelieu River to the St. Lawrence River and out to the Atlantic. When the Champlain Canal opened the southern end of the lake, cargo could travel directly from the Champlain Valley down the Hudson River to the markets of New York City and the Atlantic seaboard, and Canadian-American trade declined.

Before the canal opened, Burlington was the established wholesale center for northern Vermont and New York. Most of the occupants of Chittenden County were farmers who relied on the sale of wheat, wool and cattle for their income. Burlington merchants and exporters purchased goods in Boston or New York on credit, sold them to inland farmers at a profit, and received in payment farm products that in turn formed cargoes for their vessels. The vessels themselves, locally built, fitted out, and maintained, added another element to the local economy. In both buying and selling, merchants covered great distances, and profits depended on covering those distances rapidly and with as few transfers as possible.

After the canal opened, shipping increased dramatically. The number of commercial vessels on the lake jumped from 40 to 200 in the first years and continued to multiply. Burlington changed from a village to a bustling economic center. A tremendous variety of goods could now easily be shipped directly from or to Burlington without the expense of overland travel, making consumer goods available to a much wider population. Every spring and fall, storekeepers from surrounding communities converged on Burlington in search of bargains.

A Canal Schooner Under Sail near the Mouth of Otter Creek on Lake Champlain, circa 1888.
This photograph of a canal schooner presents the profile and sail plan of these once common freight carriers. Note the schooner's small boat being towed astern.
Courtesy Special Collections, Bailey/Howe Library, University of Vermont.

The Sailing Canal Boats of Lake Champlain

We now know that simultaneous with the opening of the Champlain Canal a new vessel type was invented, the Lake Champlain sailing canal boat.

"The vessel was built as an experiment and is found to answer all the uses intended."
—Mercantile Advertiser, September 6, 1823

In 1823, just as the Northern Canal was about to be completed and connect the waters of Lake Champlain to the Hudson River, a new vessel type was invented: the Lake Champlain sailing canal boat. The new cargo vessel was designed as an experiment. The new vessel, a hybrid able to operate on the open waters of both lakes and rivers, could also transit the restricted spaces of canals: the sailing rig was designed to be easily lowered when entering the canal, and the centerboard or leeboards, necessary while under sail, could be raised while in the canal. The size and shape of this new vessel also conformed to the dimensions of the smallest locks in the canals. With these features, the new vessel-class could carry cargo on and off the lake with speed and efficiency.

The opening of the Northern, or Champlain, Canal would connect Lake Champlain with markets along the Hudson River and New York City. The citizens and merchants of the North Country looked forward to a sudden increase in affordable trade goods, and opportunities shipping and selling them. The Burlington *Northern Sentinel* commented, "…merchandise can now be transported…to and from St. Albans in 10–14 days, and at an expense of ten dollars per ton. Hitherto the time required for carrying merchandise…has been 25 to 30 days, at an expense of 25–30 dollars per ton." The new canal would trigger the most dramatic increase in trade ever experienced in the region. New vessels would need to be rapidly built and put into service.

Map showing the regional waterways used by canal boats.

Champlain Canal Lock (handwritten on image)

Waterford, New York, Side-cut Lock, circa 1880. This photograph shows a standard canal boat being towed by a team of mules out of a canal lock. A canal boat's size and shape was dictated by the lock dimensions. Canal boats were built as large as possible, maximizing their carrying capacity, with just enough room to pass through the locks and fit within the depth of the canal.

(facing page)
Albany, circa 1825.
From a private collection.

32   Courtesy Canal Society of New York State.

Drawn by J.R. Smith.

C. A. & Co. Sc. Lancaster.

ALBANY.

New ⛵ Line of SLOOPS on *LAKE CHAMPLAIN;*

IN CONNEXION WITH THE TROY AND ERIE LINE OF SLOOPS.

SLOOPS.	MASTERS.	RESIDENCE.
Montgomery,	A. Smith,	*Whitehall, N. Y.*
Emperor Alexander,	H. Ferris,	*Chazy, N. Y.*
Gold Hunter,	A. Ferris,	*Plattsburgh, N. Y.*
Saranac,	E. Newell,	*West Port, N. Y.*
Patriot,	C. E. Barton,	*Charlotte, Vt.*
Waterloo,	A. White,	*Shelburn, Vt.*

The above sloops are all in good condition for business, all of which are new, and thoroughly repaired—and will freight from Whitehall, N. Y. and St. Johns, L. C. or any port on Lake Champlain. The respective owners and masters will hold themselves answerable, as common carriers, for damages done on board their respective vessels.

Persons desirous of favouring this line with their business, will find one of the above sloops at Whitehall, ready to receive freight.

Messrs. Ezra Smith and Asa Eddy are employed as agents at Whitehall for the company, to attend to all their business, who will, when necessary, receive property in store at satisfactory prices. Their agents have a number of excellent Canal Boats, by which they will be enabled to forward to, and receive from the Troy & Erie and Albany sloop lines, such freight as may be consigned to their care.

The New Line tender their grateful thanks for the liberal encouragement they received the last season, and hope by their unremitted attention, promptitude and despatch, to merit a further share of publick patronage.

Whitehall, March 9, 1824.

ERASTUS ADAMS, PRINTER, WHITEHALL, N. YORK.

View of Whitehall, New York, Lake Champlain, circa 1820. Detail from Plate No. 21, by Jacques Milbert, from LCMM Collection.

Traditional Lake Champlain sloops and schooners could carry freight to the new canal entrance at Whitehall (the southern end of Lake Champlain) where they transferred their cargo to standard canal boats that were towed by horses or mules through the canal. While this arrangement worked, the time and labor spent in transferring cargo added to the cost of shipment. The moment was ripe for invention. Even before the canal was completed, a few enterprising lakemen began pondering the possibilities presented by the new waterway. The result was the Lake Champlain sailing canal boat, a vessel that could sail like a traditional sloop to the entrance of the canal, and then, by having its mast unstepped and its centerboard or leeboards raised, transformed into a standard canal boat. With this capability, "property put on board at one port went through to its destination without handling." (*Vermont Historical Gazetteer,* 1867)

New Line of Sloops on Lake Champlain, 1824. This broadside reflects the dramatic increase in all forms of lake commerce after the Champlain Canal opened. From LCMM Collection.

View of New York Taken from Weahawk [Weehawken, New Jersey], circa 1820.
The opening of the Champlain Canal gave Champlain Valley merchants access
to the marketplaces all along the Hudson River and in New York City.
Plate No.1 by Jacques Milbert, From a private collection.

⊰ *Four Classes of Sailing Canal Boats* ⊱

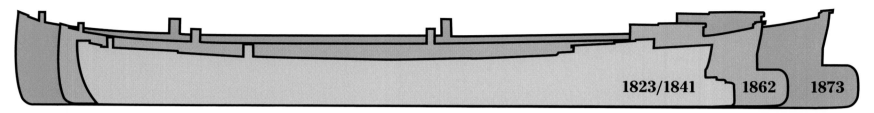

1823/1841   1862   1873

Sailing Canal Boat Profiles. The sizes of sailing canal boats increased with each expansion of the canal locks.
By Adam Loven, from LCMM Collection.

Research now suggests there were four distinct classes of sailing canal boats that are identified by the date at which they first came into use: the 1823-class, the 1841-class, the 1862-class and finally the 1873-class.

1823-Class

The earliest sailing canal boats, those built from 1823–1840, were designed both to sail efficiently on the open lake and to ride smoothly under tow through the new canal. However, the earliest 1823-class vessels were not uniform in design. Rigged either as sloops or as schooners, these boats had variations in appearance and features given to them by their respective builders. Nonetheless, they all had some common characteristics. Their masts could easily be lowered or removed at the canal entrance at Whitehall, and they were equipped with centerboards or leeboards, or shallow keels in order to function efficiently while on the lake under sail. They also needed shallow drafts, because the canal locks and canal regulations limited the overall dimensions of these canal boats to "$78^{62}/_{100}$ feet long and $14^{46}/_{100}$ feet wide."

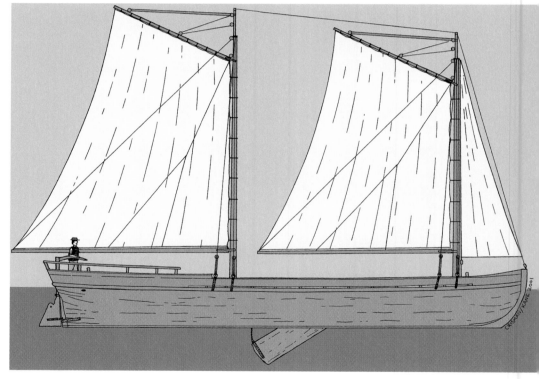

Canal Schooner **Troy.** Conjectural drawing of the canal schooner *Troy* (1825). The *Troy* is the only 1823-class sailing canal boat found in Lake Champlain.
By Kevin Crisman and Adam Kane, from LCMM Collection.

William Annesley, Pioneering Naval Architect

The men who designed and built these early sailing canal boats remain, for the most part, anonymous. One interesting exception is British naval architect William Annesley. Annesley was a pioneer in new techniques in boat construction and wrote *A New System of Naval Architecture*, published in London in 1822. In this treatise, Annesley argued that ships should be constructed "with planks and boards...which are laid in courses at right angles alternatively, longitudinal, vertical or oblique, and where curves require it, upon molds." This technique "excluded frame timbers, beams, knees, breast hooks and stem." Remarkably, in 1823, Annesley came to the Champlain Valley to sell his new methods. He achieved some success and sold at least seven patents for sailing canal boats with laminated hulls. Mathew Sax operated a busy store and commercial wharf at Chazy, New York. Sax commissioned and launched an Annesley-designed sailing canal boat, christened appropriately, *William Annesley*. Apparently well satisfied with the new vessel, Sax ordered a second later that summer. To date, no archaeological example of an Annesley vessel has been located.

A

NEW SYSTEM

OF

NAVAL ARCHITECTURE,

BY WILLIAM ANNESLEY.

LONDON:

PRINTED BY W. NICOL, SUCCESSOR TO W. BULMER AND CO.
CLEVELAND-ROW, ST. JAMES'S;
AND SOLD BY G. AND W. NICOL, PALL-MALL; J. M. RICHARDSON,
NO. 23, CORNHILL; AND J. BOOTH, DUKE-STREET,
PORTLAND-PLACE.
1822.

A

COMMENTARY

ON THE

NEW SYSTEM

OF

NAVAL ARCHITECTURE

OF

WILLIAM ANNESLEY,

ARCHITECT.

BY JOHN L. SULLIVAN.

TROY, N. Y.

PRINTED BY WILLIAM S. PARKER.
1823.

(above and left)
Title Pages from Two Annesley-Related Publications.
The original *A New System of Naval Architecture*, published in London in 1822, and *Commentary on the New System* published the following year in Troy, New York.
Courtesy, the New York Public Library and the Peabody Museum Library, Salem, Massachusetts.

(right)
Plates from A New System of Naval Architecture, *1822.*
Courtesy New York Public Library.

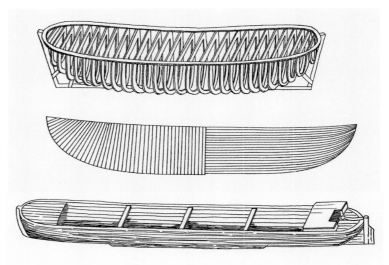

Canal Schooner **Gleaner.** This *Gleaner*, built in Champlain, New York, in 1883, is a member of the largest class of canal schooners built on Lake Champlain. This vessel was named after the original *Gleaner*, built in St. Albans, Vermont, in 1823, and the first vessel to travel through the completed Champlain Canal. From a private collection.

1823-class by the numbers
Length: 48½ to 81 feet
Beam: 13 to 13½ feet
Depth: 3¾ to 5¼ feet

Champlain Canal
Authorized: 1817
Completed: 1823
Canal Lock Dimensions:
Length: 90 feet
Width: 15 feet
Canal Prism Dimensions:
Width at top: 40 feet
Width at bottom: 26 feet
Depth: 4 feet

The Gleaner

In September 1823, *Gleaner* was the first boat to travel through the newly-completed canal. *Gleaner's* maiden voyage through the new canal evoked celebrations all along the Hudson River route to New York City. In Troy, "The city turned out to greet the arrival of the large and beautiful lake boat *Gleaner* from St. Albans…as it passed the sloop lock just above us which completes the connection to the Northern Canal with the river Hudson." An article in the *Mercantile Advertiser* of New York City described *Gleaner* in detail. "She is 35 tons custom house measurement, carries a cargo of 60 ton —is 57 feet keel, 60 feet on deck and $13^{1}/_{2}$ feet wide —has a handsome cabin, with 10 good berths for passengers…with a full cargo she will draw $3^{1}/_{2}$ feet – being six inches less than the depth of water in the canal." The same article stated, "The vessel was built as an experiment and is found to answer all the uses intended. She sails as fast and bears the changes of weather in the lake and river as well as ordinary sloops and is constructed properly for passing through the canal." *Gleaner* was a Lake Champlain sailing canal boat!

1841-Class

The 1841-class of canal boats is distinguished from earlier canal boats by the fleets of sailing canal boats which were launched by regional merchants. Firms such as Mosley D. Hall of Vergennes, Vermont, and Follett and Bradley of Burlington, created lines of sailing canal boats—all of which were built the same size and with the same type of rig. Follett and Bradley, which operated a fleet of canal sloops known as the "Merchant's Line," became the largest wholesale merchants in the Champlain Valley.

As large-scale shippers, Follett and Bradley keenly understood the advantages of the sailing canal boat in saving time and money. They also had enough capital to commit themselves to building a fleet of boats. This commitment produced the 1841-class of sailing canal boats, as others followed their lead.

Nineteenth-century observers marked the launch of the first 1841-class canal boats as the moment when traditional lake shipping began to decline. Sailing canal boats gradually came to dominate lake shipping. The older lake sloops and schooners were no longer able to compete, and they began to disappear.

Centralized management characterized this class of sailing canal boats. Typically sloop-rigged, these sturdy vessels proved economically successful. A contract for a brand new sailing canal boat "of full size for the locks…and to be of the best quality and the work and fastening to be fully equal to any boat ever built on Lake Champlain" cost Follett and Bradley fifteen hundred dollars.

1841-class by the numbers
Length: 73½ to 81 feet
Beam: 12½ to 13½ feet
Depth: 3¼ to 5¼ feet

Canal Sloop H.H. Adams, *circa 1890*. The 1841-class canal sloop was 79-feet long, 13½-feet wide and 5 feet in the hold. They generally had a sharper bow profile than the later classes. To date, no image of this class of vessel has been found, but this photograph of the *H.H. Adams,* although a larger sloop built in 1885 at Champlain, New York, provides a sense of the earlier canal sloop's appearance.
From a private collection.

1862-Class

The dramatic success of both the Champlain and Erie Canals led to an almost immediate call for their expansion so that larger canal boats carrying more cargo could travel in them. In 1835, scarcely a decade after the canals opened, their enlargement was begun. Improvements to the Erie Canal were implemented quickly, however, the enlargement of the Champlain Canal was undertaken in a more piecemeal fashion. As individual locks needed repairs they were enlarged. By 1858 all of the locks in the Champlain canal could accommodate a larger class of canal boat. However, it was not until 1862 that the expansion of the entire canal prism was completed. In the years between 1858 and 1862 the dimensions of the canal prism were too small in many places to allow two vessels to pass side by side. Canal boats would often have to wait in pull offs while boats traveling in the opposite direction passed. In some unfortunate instances a canal boat would have to be towed backwards to a pull off when boats unexpectedly met each other.

The canal boats belonging to the 1862-class date from as early as 1858 (when all of the locks were expanded) and were built until 1872 (when the next expansion of the locks was completed). The 1862-class canal boats differed in size and construction from earlier boats. The sloop rig was still the preferred sail plan for sailing canal boats, however, an increasing number of schooners also found their way onto Lake Champlain. Two of these schooners have been archaeologically studied: *General Butler* and *O.J. Walker*, built in Essex, New York, and Burlington, Vermont, respectively. Both schooners were built in 1862 and share the distinction of sinking in Burlington Bay.

Canal Schooner W.H. Roberts. The schooner was built in Essex, New York in 1862.
From a private collection.

1862-class by the numbers
Length: 83 to 87¾ feet
Beam: 13 to 15 feet
Depth: 4½ to 7¼ feet

1835 Canal Expansion
Authorized: 1835
Completed: 1862
Canal Lock Dimensions:
Length: 100 feet
Width: 15 feet
Canal Prism Dimensions:
Width at top: 50 feet
Width at bottom: 35 feet
Depth: 5 feet

1873-Class

When the first enlargement was completed in 1862 on the Champlain Canal, the next enlargement began to be promoted. The Erie Canal had been enlarged in 1835 to accommodate vessels more than 90-feet in length and 17½-feet wide. The Erie Canal locks and prism permitted vessels with drafts of seven feet that could carry over 200 tons of cargo to transit the east-west canal corridor. In 1864 the enlargement of the Champlain Canal's locks and prism was begun so that it would conform with the larger dimensions of the Erie. In anticipation of the Champlain's enlargement, several canal schooners were built to these enlarged dimensions even before the locks were completed. By 1873, even though New York State had difficulty enlarging the canal prism to beyond a depth of six feet, almost all canal boats were over 90 feet in length and 17 feet in beam. This was the last expansion of the Lake Champlain sailing canal boat.

The canal schooners were displaced for a number of reasons, the most important of which was their decreasing ability to compete with standard canal boats. As the nineteenth century progressed, the efficiency of towing canal boats on Lake Champlain with steam tugs increased. As steam tugs became more common on the lake, the cost-benefit of utilizing the wind for propulsion decreased. The expense of maintaining rigging and sails, and the reduced cargo capacity because of the centerboard in the middle of the hull, made sailing canal boats less able to compete with standard canal boats. By the 1880s, sailing canal boats, like the earlier sloops and schooners, were disappearing from the lake.

1873-class by the numbers
Length: 91½ to 99 feet
Beam: 15 to 18 feet
Depth: 6 to 8½ feet

1864 Canal Expansion
Authorized: 1864
Completed: 1877
Canal Lock Dimensions:
Length: 110 feet
Width: 18 feet
Canal Prism Dimensions:
Width at top: 65 feet
Width at bottom: 44 feet
Depth: 6 feet

1873-class Canal Schooner Hiram Walker *at Maple Street Dock in Burlington, circa 1890. The* Hiram Walker *was built in 1886 in Champlain, New York.*
Courtesy Vermont Historical Society.

❧ The Chambly Connection: The Route to Canada, 1843 ❧

The immediate success of the Champlain and Erie canals encouraged numerous other canal projects. In New York State during this period, many new canals were in the planning stages and existing canals were continually being surveyed for expansion. The success of the Champlain Canal had a devastating effect on the longstanding traditional trade activity between Lake Champlain and the Canadian markets. Before completion of the Champlain Canal, almost all Champlain Valley exports had followed the waterways north to Canada. St. Jean, Quebec, was a trading center and volumes of timber were rafted through the Richelieu River to Quebec City for export to Europe. The opening of the Champlain Canal in 1823 turned most of this commerce southward along the new, more economical canal that connected Champlain Valley entrepreneurs with vast new marketplaces.

St. Johns, Richelieu River, circa 1850.
By W.H. Bartlett, From a private collection.

42

Fort Chambly, Chambly, Quebec, circa 1850.
By W.H. Bartlett, From a private collection.

Canadian merchants were not idle. They realized their livelihood had been diverted by the Champlain Canal, and immediately began to lobby their government to build a canal to bypass the rapids on the Richelieu River between St. Jean and Chambly. Although this effort began as work started on the Champlain Canal, it was not until 1843 that the Chambly Canal was completed. The 12-mile long canal had nine locks of sufficient size to accommodate all the existing vessels engaged in New York canal shipping. Unfortunately for the Canadian canal interests, by the time the canal was completed, railroads were making their way into the same territories that the canal served. The Chambly Canal never achieved its hoped for potential, but it did provide an outlet for massive quantities of Canadian timber products to the United States. It also gave the canal boatman access to an expanded range of markets, and most of them regularly worked this extended route from New York City to the St. Lawrence and Ottawa Rivers.

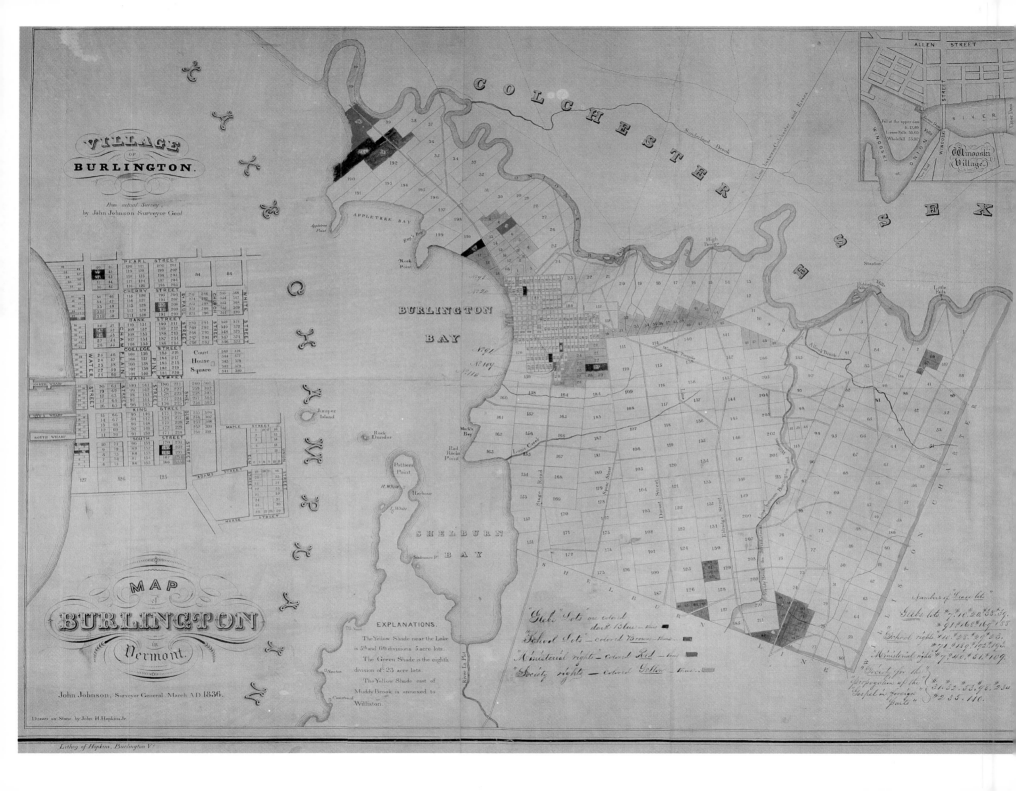

VILLAGE OF BURLINGTON.

From actual Survey
by John Johnson Surveyor Gen.l

MAP of BURLINGTON in Vermont.

John Johnson, Surveyor General. March AD 1836.

Drawn on Stone by John H. Hopkins Jr.

Lithog. of Hopkins, Burlington Vt.

COLCHESTER

ESSEX

BURLINGTON BAY

SHELBURN BAY

APPLETREE BAY

Minooski Village.

ALLEN STREET

EXPLANATIONS.

The Yellow Shade near the Lake is 5th and 6th divisions 5 acre lots.
The Green Shade is the eighth division of 25 acre lots.
The Yellow Shade east of Muddy Brook is annexed to Williston.

"Glebe" Lots are colored dark Blue — thus
"School Lots" — colored Brown — thus
"Ministerial rights" — colored Red — thus
"Society rights" — colored Yellow — thus

Numbers of "Drive lots"
Glebe lots N.o 7, 10, 20, 33, 39,
            91, 108, 169, 188
School rights N.o 10, 28, 29, 35,
            71, 189, 192, 193
Ministerial rights N.o 7, 40, 51, 109.
"Society for the
Propagation of the
Gospel in foreign
Parts" N.o 31, 32, 33, 98, 234
            2, 35, 110.

PEARL STREET
CHERRY STREET
BANK STREET
COLLEGE STREET
MAIN STREET
KING STREET
SOUTH STREET
MAPLE STREET
ADAMS STREET
MORSE STREET
WHITE STREET
CHURCH STREET
ST PAUL STREET
SHELBURN STREET
WATER STREET
CHAMPLAIN STREET
Court House Square

NORTH WHARF
STEEL'S WHARF
SOUTH WHARF

Rock Point
Juniper Island
Rock Dunder
Red Rocks Point
Potters Point
Appletree Point
Mark's Bay
Lone Creek
Shelburn Bay
Pottier's Point

Sunderland Brook
High Bridge
Little Falls
Winooski River
Winooski Village
Stage Road
Spear Street
Dorset Street
Ellisburgh Street

WINOOSKI STREET
ONION RIVER

The opening of the Northern Canal in 1823 dramatically increased maritime traffic throughout Lake Champlain. This stimulated Burlington Bay harbor improvements, some of which can still be seen. Federally-funded lighthouses replaced the informal system of private lights tended by residents. The first of these, constructed on Juniper Island in 1826, guided vessels into the port of Burlington. Another prominent improvement was the Burlington Breakwater, designed to give vessels moored in the inner harbor protection from the effects of the weather. The first section was finished in 1837, but for the next sixty years the breakwater underwent almost continuous expansion.

The lower shipping rates, however, did not translate into universal prosperity. When shipping prices went down, Vermont farmers who had relied on wheat as a cash crop suddenly found that they could no longer compete with the grain produced on the new, high-yield wheat lands in the west. Similarly, competition from the newly designed canal boats drew business away from the traditional sloops and schooners, and they gradually were abandoned.

This system of transportation [canal schooners] gradually takes the through business away from the sloops and schooners, leaving them mostly employed in freighting lumber, until the further building of them ceases. The owners of them and the "short" boats [standard canal boats] on the canal find it necessary, in order to protect themselves from the inroads which the "long boat" [sailing canal boat] system is making upon them, to build Steam freight vessels on the lake, to connect with their canal boats at Whitehall. The sloops and schooners are abandoned so far as the transportation of merchandise, produce or any property which requires speed. The result of this is the building of the "propeller" James H. Hooker in 1846, the steamboat Ethan Allen in 1847, and the Oliver Bascom in 1856.

—*Vermont Historical Gazetteer*, 1867

Burlington Bay. This engraving depicts traditional schooners sailing past the Juniper Island lighthouse with the Four Brothers Islands and the Adirondack Mountains in the background. From LCMM Collection.

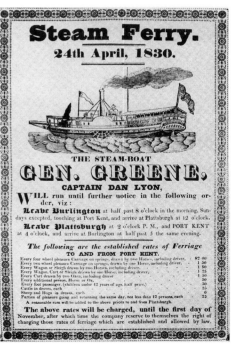

Map Burlington, Vermont, 1836. The three substantial wharves attest to the rapid development of Burlington's waterfront after the opening of the Champlain Canal. By John Johnson, courtesy City of Burlington.

Steam Ferry Gen. Greene, 1830. This broadside gave the schedule and rates for the cross-lake ferry *Gen. Greene* that began service from Burlington to Port Kent and Plattsburgh in 1825. From Ross, *Steamboats of Lake Champlain.*

45

At the same time that water-based transportation increased in speed and efficiency, travel overland also improved to move goods and passengers more efficiently to and from the waterfront. Throughout the middle decades of the nineteenth century, Burlington was a hotbed of shifting alliances and rivalries as alternative forms of transportation developed. Shipping by water competed with transport by overland horse teams on improved roads and by rail.

In the earliest days Burlington relied on horse-drawn transportation to carry goods from the waterfront to outlying communities and distant markets. Stage coach service and freight hauling by wagons required improved roads. In the winter, horse teams had more flexibility, as they could haul loaded sleighs through woods and fields or along the frozen lake. By the 1830s, many communities saw railroads as the key to increased prosperity. As early as 1832, the Vermont Railway Company was granted a charter to build a line from Burlington to the Connecticut River. This charter was not actually activated and it was December of 1849 before rail service reached Burlington. Railroads continued to expand over the next half-century, and for awhile, the rival Rutland & Burlington and Vermont Central Railroads built and maintained separate lines into the city, with passenger stations located only three blocks apart.

꧁꧂

"(The) expense of overland transportation from Montpelier to Boston is about $20 per ton. While the same freight will be taken at the wharf in Burlington and delivered to Boston for $6.50 and with but one transshipment."
—*The Burlington Free Press,* April 19, 1844

View of Burlington, circa 1853.
By Robert Sears, from a private collection.

Horse Teams

Large teams patterned after the prairie schooners, drawn by four and six horses, made trips from points as far as St. Johnsbury to Burlington, laden with loads of pelts, wheat and other farm produce, to exchange here for teas, spices, rum and other merchandise, unloaded at local wharves. It was not unusual to see 15 or 20 wagons around one of the taverns.

—"Old Burlington" by R. J. Irwin,
Burlington Free Press, May 14, 1918

Conestoga Wagon. Travel over land was much more expensive than by water.
From Dunbar, *History of Travel in America.*

Merchant, Shipper and Railroad Promoter Timothy Follett

Timothy Follett (1783–1857) experienced both the opportunities and the hazards of investing in the transportation industry. Follett, a lawyer and an 1810 University of Vermont graduate, became one of the leading merchants in the region. In 1827, he purchased an interest in the South Wharf. By 1841, he was senior partner of Follett and Bradley, a leading firm of wholesale forwarding merchants and owners of the Merchants Line of canal boats. Anticipating the future of the railroad, he sold out his interests in shipping and became president and prime mover of the Rutland & Burlington Railroad, only to lose his fortune when the railroad he founded went bankrupt in the 1850s.

Lorraine "Brecy" Farnsworth Follett and Timothy Follett, circa 1825. Portraits of Mr. and Mrs. Follett still hang on the walls of the Follett House.
Courtesy Pomerleau Real Estate.

The Timothy Follett House. Designed by Ammi Young and completed in 1841, the house is a tangible reminder of the volume of commerce and resultant wealth in Burlington during the canal and pre-railroad era.
From LCMM Collection.

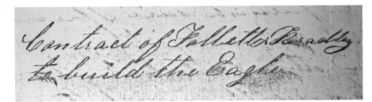

Contract of Follett & Bradley to Build Eagle. Title to a contract between Burlington shipwright Orson Spear and merchants Follett & Bradley for a canal boat "of full size for the locks" executed on October 14, 1842.
Courtesy Special Collections, Bailey/Howe Library, University of Vermont.

Line Drawings for Canal Sloops Eagle *and* Empire, *circa 1842.*
Drawn by Adam Loven from original plans by Orson Saxton Spear. From LCMM Collection.

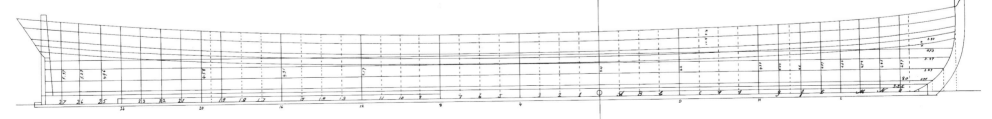

Burlington, Vt. 1846, From the Hill. This wonderful portrait of Burlington from its idyllic rural outskirts shows a prosperous village served by an active waterfront. Two steamboats and a number of sailing vessels can be seen as well as the breakwater. Note the Juniper Island Lighthouse at left.

Steam Locomotive Approaching the North End of Burlington Harbor, circa 1860. The north end of the breakwater is visible in the background, as are stacks of lumber on newly-filled land.
Courtesy Special Collections, Bailey/Howe Library, University of Vermont.

From the earliest history of the mercantile business of Burlington until [the 1850s], it had been the custom of most of the merchants throughout the county and even as far as Montpelier to order their goods of Burlington merchants. All this is changed by the new system of [rail] traffic, and the commercial importance of the town, it was feared, was ruined forever.

— W.S. Rann, *History of Chittenden County Vermont, 1886*

Long-distance shipping made up the majority of lake transportation, and rail service immediately took business away from some water-based operations. Trains offered speed, predictable schedules, and the ability to travel throughout the winter. At first, they supplemented the canal network, but as rail lines reached further, they began to bypass the older system. By the time the Civil War broke out, canal boats hauled only the heavier and less lucrative freight: coal, stone, iron ore, and lumber made up most of their cargo. At the same time, steamboats began to set their schedules so that they connected with train service. The lumber industry, relying on a combination of water and rail transportation, drove the development of Burlington's waterfront for another fifty years.

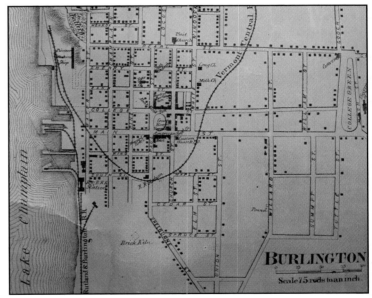

Burlington, 1860. This map depicts the original circuitous route of the Vermont Central Railroad into the city from the north.
From H.P. Wallings, 1860, from a private collection.

⚜ *Burlington Harbor in the 1850s* ⚜

This wonderful panorama of Burlington Bay was completed in about 1850. It shows the harbor with three established commercial docks at the foot of Main, King, and Maple Streets. The docks house the cranes, warehouses, and other infrastructure that made the harbor work. Burlington's skyline is dominated by its churches, the University and the recently completed mansion of Timothy Follett. Artist Joseph H. Hill, sketching from the Burlington Breakwater, chose to depict a relatively quiet day on the waterfront. He captures the masts of several sailing vessels rising behind the warehouse on King Street as well as a steamboat on the opposite side of the wharf. Today, this same pier is still used as the headquarters of the Lake Champlain Transportation Company, established in Burlington and in continuous operation since 1826.

At the south end of the harbor, a Burlington & Rutland Railroad train is shown. The railroad came to the waterfront in December 1849. The arrival of this new mode of transportation had a profound impact on Burlington Bay and the rest of the region. Railroads also had a dramatic effect on the fleet of wooden ships that had dominated the lake trade since the 1780s, eventually dooming the fleet to extinction.

Near the railroad at the south end of the harbor, the artist has shown a vessel being built parallel to the shoreline for a sideways launch. It is rigged as a sloop and likely depicts the 1841-class of sailing canal boats being built at that time by Orson Saxton Spear, Burlington's master shipwright.

Panorama of Burlington Harbor, circa 1850. Drawn by Joseph H. Hills from the breakwater. Lake Champlain historian Ralph Nading Hill admired this panorama so much that he put it on his letterhead.
From a private collection.

In the 1850s, the railroads influenced life in Burlington in many ways. Newly arrived immigrants found work building, maintaining and running the railroads. The organized transportation network enhanced the ability of Burlington merchants to deliver their goods quickly and efficiently to a wider area. The horse team trade diminished, except for express delivery services that met the trains. Some local merchants and manufacturers lost customers to producers in distant cities. Alarmed by the weakened economy, a group of prominent businessmen raised funds to build a new industry on the waterfront to stimulate employment. They established the Pioneer Mechanics Shops in 1852. Many Burlington citizens contributed to support the construction of the company's four-story, four hundred-foot long building, where a number of businesses shared steam power from two engines along a belt system. Industrial shops produced iron castings, sashes and blinds, and furniture. Fire destroyed the original structure in 1858. Pioneer Mechanics Shops immediately rebuilt, this time in three separate brick buildings, some of which survive to the present.

❦

Burlington, Vt. 1858, From the Lake. Detail showing the active waterfront and the large brick Pioneer Mechanics Shops complex. Courtesy of Shelburne Museum.

We are now prepared to inform our readers that an association (of local business men) has been formed with a view to afford facilities GENERALLY for manufacturing purposes…Instead of sending away, who knows where for everything from wooden machines and hollow ware down to our very mop handles, why should we not make all these things for ourselves!
—Pioneer Workshops, Burlington Courier, August 12, 1852

Canal Schooner with Tender, circa 1862. This photograph shows the canal schooner sail plan, as well as the always present tender. Note the faint image of a steamboat to the left of the tender.
Courtesy Special Collections, Bailey/Howe Library, University of Vermont.

⫷ *The Civil War Era in Burlington* ⫸

In 1861, the Civil War subordinated ordinary business concerns. While the battles took place far from Burlington, the conflict altered people's daily lives in many ways. Telegraph connections brought news from the battlefront, regiments of young men marched off to war, and Burlington built and adapted a hospital to care for wounded veterans. New businesses sprang up—L. Barnes & Co., with branches in Burlington, Whitehall and Montreal, manufactured "portable houses" for Army use; the Burlington Mill Company, incorporated in 1862, furnished woolen cloth for uniforms and blankets. To assist in moving troops and supplies, the military requisitioned the lake's steamboats, and railroad lines were expanded and improved. By the time the war ended, more than 34,000 Vermonters had enlisted. A quarter of them were killed or wounded, and half of the survivors never returned to live in the state. Even with peace restored, Champlain Valley families and communities would never be the same.

(above)
Twelfth Vermont Regiment, Encampment in Winter, 1862–1863.
Courtesy Special Collections, Bailey/Howe Library, University of Vermont.

(left)
General Benjamin F. Butler.
From H.D. Millholland, *Divided We Fought: A Pictorial History of the War 1861–1865.*

General Butler
Benjamin F. Butler, a Massachusetts lawyer, was given a commission early in the Civil War. After some early successes, he was placed in command of the New England troops, including the Vermont regiments. The Lake Champlain canal schooner General Butler, *built in 1862, was named in his honor. His later war years were marked by reverses, which included direct conflict with the Vermont soldiers and the Legislature. However, the boat, named at the height of his career, remained* General Butler *until she sank in 1876.*

Kilburn and Gates Cottage Furniture Manufactory, Burlington, Established 1858.
Courtesy Special Collections, Bailey/Howe Library, University of Vermont.

⊰ After the War ⊱

With the end of the Civil War, Burlington business boomed. Steamboat lines and railroads campaigned to attract tourists, and the Champlain Valley's Revolutionary War sites and beautiful scenery made it a favorite destination. Huge vacation hotel resorts and camps appeared along the waterfront. Traffic on the lake included increasing numbers of small recreational boats.

Burlington was incorporated as a city in 1865, and the working waterfront continued to expand to accommodate the burgeoning lumber industry. Even the shape of the land itself was altered. The federally-funded breakwater sheltering the inner harbor was under almost continuous expansion, and venture capitalists built new sawmills, planing mills, box factories, docks, and railroad depots. When available empty space disappeared, extensive landfill operations added valuable waterfront acreage. Soil, sand, and gravel scooped from the neighboring hillsides established new support platforms for the stacks of lumber. The natural wetland area known as "The Cove" was dredged and converted into the Barge Canal. By 1869 the lumber industry occupied twelve wharves and acres of waterfront, including newly created filled land.

Recreational use of the waterfront diversified to include not only the passive enjoyment of admiring the scenery by tourists but also active involvement in pleasure boating by area residents. In 1885, the Lake Champlain Ice Boating Club was organized, and two years later the Lake Champlain Yacht Club was founded. Members built a clubhouse which opened the following year. In 1894, Captain Henry Chiott installed a four-horsepower gas engine in his pleasure yacht, the first gasoline-powered inboard motor boat on Lake Champlain.

The amount of lumber piled upon the wharves of our city yesterday is estimated at twenty five million feet…Burlington, as a lumber mart, is now the third, if not the second city in importance in the United States, Chicago first and Albany second.
—*Burlington Times*, December 23, 1865

Burlington Waterfront After the Fire, 1870s.
Courtesy Special Collections, Bailey/Howe Library, University of Vermont.

Lumberyards at the Burlington Waterfront, circa 1870. Looking south from Battery Park, most of what is seen is filled land, created during the lumber boom years of the mid-nineteenth century. The College Street pier is visible, but the distinctive Burlington Boathouse had not yet been built. Much of this site is today a public park.

Courtesy Special Collections, Bailey/Howe Library, University of Vermont.

⊰ *Lumber Becomes King* ⊱

During the first half of the nineteenth century, the Champlain Valley forests were heavily logged. A major part of Burlington's wealth came from the sale of lumber and the manufacture of products made from local wood. However, by mid-century, open farmlands with grazing sheep spread throughout the Champlain Valley, and most trees of any useful size were gone. In 1893, Lucius Chittenden reminisced, "You could travel now for miles in this region and not find a tree large enough to make a respectable fish pole." The Chambly Canal opened in 1843 and sparked a new era of prosperity based on lumber not from Champlain Valley forests, but imported from Canada.

Clearing Up A Farm, circa 1880. The Champlain Valley forest so coveted by European explorers and settlers gradually disappeared under their axes and saws. Much of the timber was used for shipbuilding both here and away, but vast quantities were cut for charcoal manufacturing for the growing iron industry. By the middle of the nineteenth century, most of the region's prime forests were gone.
By Rowland E. Robinson, courtesy of Rokeby Museum.

Shepard and Davis Lumber Yard, Burlington, circa 1880. Burlington earned a new lease on commercial life by importing vast quantities of Canadian lumber via the Chambly Canal.
From a private collection.

Now trade on the lake was evenly balanced between northern and southern connections. Burlington remained the hub. Large Canadian barges, called *pin plats*, each carrying 80,000 feet of lumber, loaded at the mills at Ottawa, Three Rivers, and other lumber towns in Canada. They sailed or were towed to Burlington via the St. Lawrence, the Richelieu River and the Chambly Canal. Piles of lumber thirty or forty feet high covered more than thirty acres of the Burlington waterfront. Lumber left Burlington daily via the Vermont Central and Rutland Railroads, bound for cities all over New England.

Canadian Pin Plat, Octave *of Montreal, circa 1880.* The pin plat was a distinctively shaped and rigged Canadian cargo carrier.
Courtesy Isle La Motte Historical Society.

The pin plat business here has been quite dull lately...the pin plat is a native of Canada and looks like an old-fashioned country woodbox magnified fifty times.
—*Burlington Free Press and Times,* July 7, 1871

Dock Scene, Burlington, Vt. Shows three Canadian pin plats tied up at one of Burlington's dock.
From LCMM Collection.

(right)
Burlington, Marble Works, Established 1865. This image of the Burlington Marble Works shows the transportation network in action. Stone is delivered and shipped out by boat and rail, smaller products such as monuments and architectural elements are carried by wagons and a variety of period watercraft. At the left side of the image, the barge canal entrance with two sections of the breakwater and the railroad lift-bridge can be seen. The Burlington breakwater with a steamboat passing by its southern light can also be seen.
Reprint published by WCAX, courtesy Paul Bruhn.

PUBLISHED BY WCAX-TV
BURLINGTON, VERMONT

BURLINGTON MF'G. CO. MARBLE WORKS

OFFICE

MARBLE WORKS, BURLINGTON, VT.
1865

BIRDS EYE VIEW OF
BURLINGTON
AND
WINOOSKI VT.

SHOBER & CARQUEVILLE, CHICAGO

DRAWN BY E.MEILBEK   PUBLISHED BY J.J. STONER MADISON WIS.

BURLINGTON REFERENCES.

1 U. S. Custom House and Post Office.
2 City Hall.
3 Court Hall.
4 University of Vermont.
5 High School and Grammar School.
6 Public School.
7 Fletcher Library.
8 County Jail.
9 Railroad Depot.
10 Steam Boat Landing.

HOTELS.

11 VanNess House, D. C. Barber & Co., Props.
12 American House, W. F. Page, Prop.
13 Park House, H. H. Pike, "
14 Rowe's Hotel, R. C. Rowe, "
15 Lake View House, A. Duguay, "

CHURCHES.

16 St. Paul's Episcopal Church.
17 First Cong. Unitarian "
18 "   Calvanistic "
19 Third Cong Calvanistic Church
20 Methodist "
21 Baptist "
22 "   French, Mission "
23 Roman Catholic, St. Mary's Cathedral.
24 "   (French) St. Joseph's Church.
25 St. Patrick's Academy, Ladies' School.
26 Roman Catholic Cemetery.
27 Ethan Allen's Monument, Green Mount Cemetery.
28 City Market.

30 City Water Works.
31 Reservoir.
32 Kilburn & Gates' Furniture Factory.
33 B. S. Nichols & Co.'s Pioneer Shops.
33 Taft & Morgan's Door, Sash & Frame Factory, in Pioneer Buildings.
34 Shepard, Morse & Co.'s Lumber Mills.
35 C. Blodgett, Son & Co., Lumber Mills.
35 Jas MacLaren, Lumber Co., Blodgett's Mills
36 Bronsman, Weston, Dunham & Co.'s Lumber Mills.

37 L. Barns, Son & Co., Lumber Co., Lumber Mills.
A   "   "   Marble Works.
A Linsley & Co.'s Lumber Mills.
38 Mathews & Nichols's Box Factory.
39 Burlington Cotton Mills, H. W. Barrett, Agt.
40 Burlington Flouring Mills, F. C. Kennedy, Agt.
"   Woolen Mills, Winooski, "
41 A. R. Buccles' Candy Factory.
43 Walker, Bro. & Co.'s Marble Works.
44 Eureka Sap Spout Manufactory.

45 Gas Works.
46 Edwards & Stevens' Machine Shops, Winooski
47 Stevens' House, J. W. Cetley, Prop.
48 Roman Catholic Church, Winooski.
49 "   "   French.
50 Episcopal Church, Winooski
51 Congregational "   "
52 Methodist "   "
53 Mount Mansfield.
54 Camels Hump.

Three Canal Boats at Burlington Harbor, circa 1880.
Courtesy Vermont Historical Society.

(left)
Birds Eye View of Burlington and Winooski, Vermont, 1877. This wonderful illustration captures the dynamics of a vibrant waterfront. Much new land has been created for lumber yards by filling in the lakefront. To the bottom right, the once "miasmic frog pond" has been converted into a boat basin by dredging the wetland.
Courtesy Fletcher Free Library.

61

Steamer Vermont II, *circa 1875*. Built at the Shelburne Shipyard, the *Vermont II* began service in 1871 and worked the lake until she retired in 1903. The *Vermont II* may have been the most beautiful steamer ever to cruise Lake Champlain.
Courtesy Vermont Historical Society.

✥ *Lumber, Ice, Oil—Let the Good Times Roll* ✥

A national financial panic from 1873–1877 slowed business on the waterfront. In 1877 the port of Burlington accommodated only 36 million feet of lumber, down from 123 million in 1873. After 1877, the quantities gradually increased, until once again the wharves and warehouses overflowed with lumber, coal, grain, salt, and general merchandise. In the 1880s, a new storage facility appeared on the waterfront when Standard Oil Company of Burlington constructed four oil storage tanks. The city also became a center for the ice industry. In 1892, the Burlington Ice Company, located at Battery and Maple Streets, dug a tunnel and belt system to convey up to 800 tons of ice a day from the frozen lake to the warehouse, where an elevator hoisted it to the upper floors. During the excavation, a temporary stable for horses and dormitory for workers were set up at the lake.

(above)
Ice House, circa 1900. In the days before electric-powered refrigeration, all cooling was done by natural ice, harvested in winter. Burlington, by benefit of its location on Lake Champlain and its rail connections, became a major source of ice.
From a private collection.

Ice Harvesting on Burlington Bay, circa 1900. "Consumers Ice Company has begun gathering ice cut about one half mile outside the breakwater for domestic purposes. It will take 60 men and 20 teams of horses about 20 days to cut the annual crop of some 60,000 tons."
Burlington Free Press and Times, February 1, 1893.
From a private collection.

❧ *The Commercial Era Fades—Recreation Rises* ❧

Schooner Scow Loaded with Lumber, circa 1890.
Courtesy Shelburne Museum.

In the mid-1890s, national economic policies abruptly undercut the prosperity of the city of Burlington. The 1893–1894 tariff changes on lumber imported from Canada reduced the quantity coming into the country, and also made it economical for Canadian yards to ship from Ottawa and other points of origin directly to Boston, New York, and other cities, without a halt in Burlington for processing. Most of the planing mills in Burlington closed. Another Congressional act put wool on the free list, threatening the survival of area woolen mills. The waterfront went into a decline.

The Lake Champlain Yacht Club's First Burlington Headquarters, circa 1890. The clubhouse formally opened in 1888.
From a private collection.

Shipping News: Port of Burlington

Some idea of the amount of business done at our wharves may be gained from the fact that the arrival of vessels during the season ending this last November, were 2563. They landed here, among other things, 60,000,000 feet of lumber and 1,000,000 bushels of grain.
—*Burlington Free Press,* January 4, 1866

The whole number of feet of lumber received at Burlington during 1868 was about 112 million, making the total business of our city for that year upwards of three million of dollars…Number of canal boat loads received: 475, Number of railroad car loads shipped: 3,778
—*Burlington Free Press,* February 6, 1869

The rates for towing through Lake Champlain this year, are lower than have been known in a long time. The lines charge but five dollars for towing from Whitehall to St. John's. This is fun for the boatmen, but death to the lines.
—*Burlington Free Press and Times,* May 22, 1876

(right)
Sandolphon, *Launched 1898.* Built in Burlington by Joseph and Alfred Richards for Alvaro Adsit, she won many races. After being converted to power, she finished her career on the Hudson River.
From LCMM Collection.

Part III

A Waterfront In Transition

The Twentieth Century

*Standard Canal Boat Approaching the
Lake Champlain Yacht Club, circa 1890.*
From a private collection.

The Twentieth Century
A Waterfront In Transition

With the imposition of a federal tariff on imported Canadian lumber, Burlington's reign as the lumber capital of the northeast ended. What could replace the thousands of board feet of timber brought by the colorful Canadian pin plat freight boats? Soon the filled land where lumber had been piled during the second half of the nineteenth century had oil stored in enormous tanks to heat the homes of the region and fuel the newest evolution of transportation technology, the automobile. As the lumber companies began to disappear from the waterfront, oil tanks and empty spaces took their place. The transition was not particularly smooth or well managed, and the once vibrant Burlington commercial waterfront became a broken down remnant of its previous self.

The transition into the new century brought other casualties as well. The steamboats had evolved into large and refined vessels and had adapted their routes to coincide with railroad schedules. In the twentieth century steamboats would finally succumb to competition from the diesel engine. The wooden fleet of Lake Champlain's commercial craft lost more and more ground to the railroads and like their cousins the steamboats, began to disappear from view. The Great Depression in the 1930s was the last straw in the demise of this once vibrant way of life.

After World War II, from the ashes of the waterfront's former activities, the community began to redefine itself. The steamboats reluctantly accepted their fate and retired from lake service to be replaced by large diesel ferries. Oil tanks, serviced by barges and tugs coming via the Champlain Canal, continued their dominant waterfront presence, but a new public consciousness about the waterfront and its potential was beginning to emerge. The use of the Burlington waterfront for recreational purposes was an idea whose time was coming, and the city debated the conversion of the old Salt Dock at the foot of Maple Street into a public park.

The last two decades of the twentieth century saw the transformation of the Burlington waterfront into a vibrant public venue. The oil tanks began to disappear, a salvage yard was relocated, and acres of filled land were transferred back to the city to become parkland. The city recreated the Burlington Community Boathouse at the foot of College Street to provide more public access to the waterfront. Where a century before stacks of lumber stood piled high, a bike and pedestrian path was established. Many of the waterfront's surviving historic buildings were adapted for new uses. As of this writing, in 2003, the trend is continuing and appears to be accelerating. The waterfront is getting new public and private investment, all tailored to transform this once working shoreline into a vibrant place for residents and visitors alike.

The Lake Champlain Maritime Museum is pleased to play a part in this transformation through its Burlington Schooner Project. We hope that construction of the canal schooner *Lois McClure* will provide a tangible reconnection between the present day waterfront and Burlington's and Lake Champlain's commercial era.

Champlain Tercentenary Celebration, Burlington, 1909.
A huge crowd gathers on College Street to mark the 300th anniversary of Champlain's arrival. Note that the original Lake Champlain Yacht Club (left) has burned and has been replaced with a new structure.
Courtesy Special Collections, Bailey/Howe Library, University of Vermont.

⚞ *Economics Redefine the Waterfront* ⚟

In the late nineteenth century, concerned citizens and wealthy philanthropists realized the special attraction of the waterfront and organized activities to celebrate its magnetism with winter sports festivals, sailing races, and commemorative events. These piecemeal attempts to enhance the waterfront, however, did not trigger any grand scheme to clean up the whole area.

The lake [once] was a busy and bustling place, dotted over with lines of canal boats, rafts of logs, and vessels under sail and steam. All this has now practically disappeared. The visitor to the lake today will see at rare intervals a solitary line of canal boats. [More often the visitor] will see nothing but a large expanse of water backed by blue mountains and intercepted here and there by groups of islands.

—Marshall O. Leighton, *Report on the Pollution of Lake Champlain,* 1905

In Tow Down Lake Champlain, circa 1900.
From LCMM Collection.

The Decline, Transition, and Renaissance of the Burlington Waterfront

As the twentieth century began, the waterfront earned a reputation as a deteriorating place in transition. Railroads, canal boats, and steamboats had managed to coexist for decades. The coming of the automobile shifted traffic decisively to land, and Burlington, like many other communities in the Champlain Valley, began to turn away from the waterfront. In the new age of motor transportation, the lake was often seen as an obstacle more than an asset. Although the new pathway to prosperity would be a network of paved roads traveled by cars and trucks, the Burlington waterfront and the Champlain Canal still had useful roles to play.

At one time, it seemed that railroads would make the Champlain Canal obsolete. A commission, appointed to consider whether the canal should be abandoned, reported back in 1903 that the canal should actually be enlarged to allow the passage of much larger vessels. Confident that the canal would continue in use, the State of New York began to deepen the channel to twelve feet, and to enlarge the locks so that they could admit vessels carrying from 300 to 600 tons. The improvements were completed in 1916. By the 1930s, most of the barges passing from the Hudson River to Lake Champlain now carried oil and gasoline. Millions of gallons were stored at ever-enlarging tank farms on the filled land once occupied by lumber yards.

Burlington at Sunset From Battery Park, circa 1900. The early twentieth century saw a declining volume of commercial harbor traffic.
Courtesy Special Collections, Bailey/Howe Library, University of Vermont.

Dredge Enlarging the Champlain Canal, Which Became Known as the New York State Barge Canal, circa 1915.
From LCMM Collection.

Waterfront Fire, 1913. The Burlington waterfront repeatedly suffered catastrophic fires.
From a private collection.

Coal Docks, Burlington, circa 1890. Shipping Pennsylvania coal via the Hudson River north to Lake Champlain and Canada was an important cargo for the canal boat trade. As the twentieth century advanced, even this freighting opportunity began to diminish. From a private collection.

The shift to land-based transportation continued. At the time of the 1903 canal survey, coal from Pennsylvania was an important maritime cargo, but by 1905, Citizens Coal Co. on Pine Street changed to handling its coal by rail. Ice harvested from the lake could also be transported by rail, and lumber shipments to Burlington were declining. By 1911, barges of hay exceeded deliveries of lumber. When a catastrophic lakefront fire in 1913 destroyed the Shepherd and Morse Co. mill and several million feet of lumber, more than 125 men were thrown out of work.

J.G. Witherbee and a Yacht at the King Street Dock, circa 1890.
J.G. Witherbee was built in Essex, New York, in 1863.
Courtesy Vermont Historical Society.

Burlington Vt. Yacht Club and Harbor, circa 1910. After the first yacht club burned in 1901, this new clubhouse was built to replace it.
From LCMM Collection.

At the same time, there was a growing interest in recreational use of the lake. As early as 1900, citizens urged city authorities to acquire waterfront property and construct a public dock. The Lake Champlain Yacht Club continued to prosper, and power boats were growing in popularity. In 1911, the American Power Boat Association of New York urged the adoption of signal flags to be used at Burlington and other ports where pleasure boats could obtain fuel. In 1916, the first effort to list boat names and owners showed several thousand motorboats plying the lake; by 1918 an act of Congress required them to be registered.

United States Customs Boat Patrol, 1927. This on-lake force operated from 1924 until 1933 to enforce the Prohibition amendment.
From a private collection.

75

The Harbor at King Street, circa 1920. The steamboats *Ticonderoga* and *Chateaugay* share the dock with barges, tugs, and pleasure craft.
Courtesy Lake Champlain Transportation Company.

Hard Hat Divers Installing a New Water Line, circa 1908. As Burlington's population increased, drinking water from the lake became more polluted. Eventually, Burlington extended its water intake line out into the bay to escape the influence of near shore sewage discharge.
Courtesy Special Collections, Bailey/Howe Library, University of Vermont.

Cleaning up the waterfront and improving water quality began to emerge as public concerns early in the century. The filtration of lakewater for drinking began in 1908, and because of sewage being released into the lake just offshore, ice companies were required to take their harvest from outside the breakwater. Plans for a year-round fish hatchery in Burlington were under discussion in 1919, and in 1920 the hatchery on Steamboat Wharf was doing big business.

Automobile Crossing on a Ferry, circa 1920.
From a private collection.

Evolution of Transportation Technology Continues— Planes, Trains, and Automobiles

In the decade after the end of World War I, Burlington experienced a building boom. Immigrants provided labor, and federal dollars encouraged the state to invest in the construction of highways and airports. The city expanded with new ties to the national economy, credit and transportation networks. It was a time of transition. The new highways encouraged more people to use private cars for recreation, and trucks took over the hauling of freight. One last schooner, the *Nelson W. Fiske*, could still be seen carrying cargo on the lake. A seaplane headquartered in Burlington in the summer of 1920 was seen as a novelty, but by 1923 Burlington was home port for many seaplanes, and the Vermont Air Transport Company anticipated using the "flying boats" on a New York to Montreal line. The major water-based transportation companies struggled to adapt to serious competitors on land. The Burlington Steam Packet Company sent out an appeal for southbound cargo. The Champlain Transportation Company boasted that its summer auto ferry between Burlington and Port Kent would save ninety miles for autoists bound for the Adirondacks. The ferries were popular, but the company was forced to discontinue steamboat excursions for lack of patronage.

Steamer Vermont III *Passing Under the Champlain Bridge, circa 1930.* The high center arch on the new Champlain Bridge was designed to allow the tall stacks of the steamboats to pass underneath. Few realized that after more than a century of success, the steamboats were approaching the end of their viability as a means of transportation. Courtesy Special Collections, Bailey/Howe Library, University of Vermont.

Seaplanes at Essex, New York, circa 1925. From LCMM Collection.

The automobile era in Vermont received an unexpected boost in 1927. Violent thunderstorms washed out roads and bridges in a great flood. A combination of local and federal money was invested in repairs, and many miles of dirt and gravel roads were given hard pavement for the first time. At the same time, planning and design work began for the Champlain Bridge, which would cross the lake from Crown Point, New York, to Chimney Point, Vermont. When the bridge opened in August 1929, for the first time in history, the Champlain Valley had a transportation link between east and west shores that was accessible at all times and all seasons.

Union Station, circa 1930. As the twentieth century began, lake transportation businesses struggled to hold onto customers. Rail service continued to serve the waterfront, and in 1916 Burlington's new Union Station opened. One of Elisha Goodsell's ferries can be seen near the third Lake Champlain Yacht Club in the background.
From a private collection.

Burlington Harbor, circa 1900. In this early twentieth century photograph, a lone canal schooner can be seen on the right. Although lake shippers tried to remain competitive, transportation by rail, land and air gradually took over.
Courtesy Special Collections, Bailey/Howe Library, University of Vermont.

Railroads Sink the Commercial Fleet

This is, next to one, the dullest season in the history of the lumber business on Lake Champlain so far as the shipments of lumber by water into Burlington goes, and less than 30 boats have been unloaded in the harbor thus far this year. There was one year shortly after the war when there was no building and fewer than 30 boats were unloaded during the season. There remain only a few weeks before the closing of navigation and there is no likelihood of the cargoes numbering much more than 30. It was only a few years ago that the ordinary year was four times what it now is, and 15 or 20 years ago the number of boats reached ten or more times the pres-

ent number. Few if any new barges are being built, and when an old boat goes, there is none to replace it. The lessening of the traffic has affected the number of tugs and they are declining in number in about the same ratio as the barges. One tug now is plying the waters where three formerly did. No coal is being received by water now, although all of the coal concerns have facilities for handling coal shipped by water. What is true of coal is true of other commodities. Shipments by rail are made to the doors of the warehouse or coal pockets and there is a big saving in the costs of handling shipments.

—Burlington Free Press, Nov. 2, 1926

Champlain Transportation Company Ferry Schedule, 1930. Although steamboat excursions declined as more people traveled by car, crossing the lake by ferry appealed to motorists and the CTC began to try to adapt to this new market.
From LCMM Collection.

79

⇥ *Steamboats Struggle to Survive* ⇥

The steamboats in service at the start of the twentieth century had not been designed to carry automobiles, but owners made efforts to keep them in use. In 1906, *Ticonderoga*, the last of the Lake Champlain steamboats, was launched at Shelburne Shipyard. She was capable of carrying a small number of cars, carefully driven onto her main deck. World War I curtailed both manufacturing and shipping, as part of the national war effort to conserve coal and lumber. After the war, the Champlain Transportation Company modified its steamboat *Chateaugay* to ferry automobiles from Burlington to Port Kent through the 1920s; a competing line, run by Elisha Goodsell, operated a rag-tag ferry fleet of three former yachts, *Oneida*, *Legonia*, and *Admiral*, from the foot of College Street in Burlington to Port Douglas, New York.

Only a few months after the festive opening of the Champlain Bridge came the economic crash that started the Great Depression. Tourist travel and excursions virtually ceased, and manufacturing slowed, further crippling Burlington's already struggling waterfront. In 1933, the Champlain Transportation Company (CTC), which had operated steamboat service continuously for over a century, suspended boat service. For the next few years, Daniel Loomis, CTC General Manager, labored to operate the steamers as excursion boats, but they simply could not compete. To operate the steamboat *Vermont III* took fifty-two hands, while

Goodsell's Ferry Dock, circa 1932. This photograph of Elisha Goodsell's operation at the foot of College Street shows his three converted steam yachts during the winter.
Photograph by McAllister of Burlington, courtesy Special Collections, Bailey/Howe Library, University of Vermont.

Ferry Landing, Burlington, circa 1933. By this time, the third Lake Champlain Yacht Club building had fallen into disrepair and was condemned by the city. In 1933, the Champlain Transportation Company announced it would not operate that season, although *Chateaugay* was leased and operated by individuals. In this photograph, Goodsell's operation is having a bad day as his ferry *Admiral* has sunk at the dock. *Chateaugay* can be seen passing in the background.
Photograph by McAllister of Burlington, courtesy Special Collections, Bailey/Howe Library, University of Vermont.

Steamer Chateaugay, *circa 1910*. Launched in 1888, the *Chateaugay* was the first iron-hulled ferry built by the Champlain Transportation Company.
Courtesy Special Collections, Bailey/Howe Library, University of Vermont.

Steamer Chateaugay *as a Car-ferry, circa 1925*. Struggling to adapt to the automobile age, *Chateaugay* was retrofitted to carry cars.
From LCMM Collection.

a new diesel steamer could manage with a crew of only three. In 1936 and 1937, Horace W. Corbin came to Burlington and built two large, welded-steel diesel ferries, *City of Burlington* and *City of Plattsburgh*. These new "streamline ferries," specifically designed to carry automobiles, proved very successful. Corbin then purchased many of the old steamers and wooden ferries of the Champlain Transportation Company. The boom in recreational travel he had anticipated was slow to materialize. The steamer *Vermont III* sat unused at Shelburne Shipyard; *Chateaugay* was sold off, cut into pieces and shipped by rail to Lake Winnipesaukee, in New Hampshire, to replace an excursion steamer destroyed by fire.

Battery-operated lights installed on the Burlington Breakwater in 1938 signaled a new optimism for the waterfront. Up until that date, local citizens had tended the light, traveling out by boat every evening to light the kerosene-fueled lamps, and returning in the morning to extinguish them. James Wakefield tended the light for over eighteen years, and Edgar Chiott for thirty years. On the final night before the automated system went into operation, an informal gathering of seventy-five people in twelve boats escorted light keeper Rolla W. Hill to shore, while a crowd of people gathered in Battery Park to witness the end of an era.

As if some blight had passed over Lake Champlain, activity along that water highway seemed to wilt and die.

STEAMER
TICONDEROGA
AT BURLINGTON, VT

Steamer Ticonderoga *at the King Street Dock in Burlington, Vt., 1929.*
Courtesy Special Collections, Bailey/Howe Library, University of Vermont.

Aerial View of Burlington Waterfront, 1929. From left, note the water plant surrounded by open land with no lumber storage, in center, the third Burlington/Yacht Club building, Union Station, with lumber stacked around King Street dock, Perkins Pier with warehouse buildings and slips for coal barges coming to the Elias Lyman Coal facilities.
From a private collection.

High Hopes for Lake Travel

As if some blight had passed over Lake Champlain, activity along that water highway seemed to wilt and die. First went the white sails that had taken the wind in their stride. Then went the splendid line steamers to be tied up to a wharf in some harbor in silent desuetude. The edict had gone forth that their day was done…

This year, however, we have reason to feel that our lake has taken a new lease on life. People who had given up hope of ever taking a trip through the waters they loved, people who regretted the fact that their children could never enjoy the thrill of a boat ride through the beautiful lake, as in their youth, are again beginning to feel that lake coming into its own…To H. W. Corbin and to him alone we must be thankful for the restoration of traffic upon the lake. Not content with building two of the most modern and serviceable of automobile ferries, he has bought the vessels of the Champlain Transportation Company and this season has put the handsome and commodious steamer Ticonderoga back into service as an excursion boat…Every lover of Lake Champlain should give a vote of thanks to Mr. Corbin because through him the lake and its people have again come into their own.

—*Plattsburgh Daily Press,* August 27, 1937

City of Plattsburgh *Launch Day, July 21, 1937.* Built at the site of the present day U.S. Coast Guard Station in Burlington, *City of Plattsburgh* joined Corbin's *City of Burlington* in cross-lake ferry service.
Photograph by McAllister of Burlington, from LCMM Collection.

Waterfront in Transition, circa 1937. By this time, the Goodsell operation was over and a new operator, Horace Corbin, was poised to take control of Burlington's ferry service. His Streamline Ferries *City of Burlington* (1936) and *City of Plattsburgh* (1937) were powered by diesel engines and specifically designed to carry cars. In 1937, he was able to purchase the ailing Champlain Transportation Company. In this photograph, *City of Burlington* is at the College Street dock as the steamer *Ticonderoga* passes in the background.
Courtesy Lake Champlain Transportation Company.

Ferry City of Burlington *Underway, circa 1936.* The Streamline Ferries *City of Burlington* and *City of Plattsburgh* operated on Lake Champlain until the war years. *City of Plattsburgh* was sold and used as a ferry in New York harbor. *City of Burlington* was sold to the Commonwealth of Virginia, where it is still in operation.
Courtesy Lake Champlain Transportation Company.

Steamer Chateaugay *on the Shelburne Shipyard's Marine Railway, 1940.*
Today, the hull of *Chateaugay* still plies the waters as the *Mt. Washington.*
Photograph by McAllister of Burlington, from the Aske Collection, LCMM.

*"Down on the shores of Shelburne Harbor today a drizzling rain wept
quiet tears on the iron hull of the old* Chateaugay, *awaiting dissection
into 20 pieces for shipment overland to Lake Winnipesaukee"*
Burlington Daily News, April 4, 1940.

Derelict Waterfront, circa 1939. The Lake Champlain Yacht Club's third clubhouse is in the
upper left. The pier approaching the clubhouse forms the northern rim of a harbor area in
which sunken derelict vessels can been seen adjacent to some houseboats. The area looks
overgrown and neglected, a sad contrast to the bustling lumberyards of earlier days.
Courtesy Special Collections, Bailey/Howe Library, University of Vermont.

❦ *World War II* ❧

Burlington from Battery Park, 1940. This photograph was taken to help illustrate a prospectus designed to entice government contracts to the area.
From the Aske Collection, LCMM.

America's entry into World War II in December 1941 provided opportunities to overcome the region's economic slump. The Queen City Cotton Mill, which had closed its doors in 1939, was leased to Bell Aircraft in 1943. Manufacturing for defense industries brought new vigor to the city during World War II and the Korean War. Although wartime rationing curtailed automobile travel, Virginia and New York City needed ferries, and Horace Corbin was able to sell his Streamline Ferries off the lake for a profit. *Ticonderoga* was pressed into service as a substitute ferry on the lake.

In 1942, the Champlain Transportation Company leased the Shelburne Shipyard to the Donovan Construction Company of Minnesota, and they secured a contract to construct ships for the U.S. Navy. During the last three years of the war, shipyard workers were busy building five 110-foot long subchasers, four tugboats, and several torpedo barges at Shelburne Shipyard. When the vessels were launched, they made their way through the Champlain Canal and south to the Navy Yards of New York City.

Aerial View of the Shelburne Shipyard, 1940.
The key to Burlington's bid to build ships for the war effort was the Shelburne Shipyard. The prospectus lists all the shipbuilding equipment on-site and especially the community of skilled labor available. "The employees at the present time are all key men of the wood and steel ship construction industry, some were born and raised at Shelburne Harbor."
From the Aske Collection, LCMM.

Launching Day for SC 1029 and SC 1030, August 31, 1942.
The first two subchasers completed were *SC 1029* and *SC 1030*.
Both did convoy duty across the Atlantic and then had
active military careers in the Mediterranean.
Photograph by McAllister of Burlington, Aske Collection, LCMM.

Shelburne Shipyard Yard Tugs, 1943. Workers pose with four YT's (yard tugs) on the marine railway being made ready to be launched all together.
Photograph by McAllister of Burlington, Aske Collection, LCMM.

⊰ *The Shelburne Shipyard* ⊱

Burlington has long benefited from its proximity to the protected bay at the end of Shelburne Point that became home to one of the lake's principal shipyards. The family of Nathan White moved to the point in 1797 and established the shipyard. Nathan's sons Robert, Andrew, and Lavater were all prominent lake captains. In 1820, the Lake Champlain Steamboat Company, then headquartered in Vergennes, purchased a portion of White's Harbor to better position their operations. From that time on, the Shelburne Shipyard became the dominant shipyard for building and maintaining steamboats on Lake Champlain and Lavater White became the principal steamboat builder for more than half a century.

In the twentieth century, as steamboating declined, so did the fortunes of the shipyard. During World War II, however, the facilities of the Shelburne Shipyard helped revitalize the greater Burlington economy. At the outbreak of the war the region's economy was in trouble and its skilled workforce was migrating to jobs on the coast. Meanwhile, across

the country in St. Paul, Minnesota, the Donovan Construction Company was also struggling because of the war. Donovan's, a rural electrification company, began to search for a government-approved shipyard that would allow them to bid on military contracts. That search brought them to the Shelburne Shipyard.

During the war, the shipyard produced five 110-foot subchasers, four tugboats and other craft to support the war effort and help sustain the local economy. The shipyard employed hundreds of skilled craftsman from around the region and subcontracted to other Burlington companies. After the war the shipyard was divided into two marinas to service expanding recreational boating activity. The Crandall marine railway remained under the control of the Lake Champlain Transportation Company (LCTC) to service its fleet of ferryboats. During the Korean War, the shipyard was used again for military shipbuilding. Today, the Griswold and Aske families continue to operate successful marinas in what was once known as White's Bay.

(left)
Subchaser 1504 *with* Ticonderoga, *1944.*
The Donavan Company built *SC 1504*, *SC 1505*, and *SC 1506* in 1944. They were the last of the World War II vessels to be built at the Shelburne Shipyard and they were reportedly all lost in a violent typhoon en route to Russia.
Courtesy Thomas H. Ouellette Family.

(below)
Vermont III *and* Ticonderoga, *circa 1945.* By the end of the war, it was clear that the old steamer *Vermont III* had become a liability. She was stripped of her superstructure, converted to diesel power, and sold for use as a coastal freighter. In the postwar years, *Ticonderoga* continued to search for a viable niche.
Courtesy Thomas H. Ouellette Family.

Ferry Valcour, *circa 1950*. Shortly after the end of World War II, the Shelburne Shipyard built the car ferry that was christened *Valcour*. Note the steamboat *Ticonderoga* at the College Street pier in the background. Courtesy Richard Wadhams.

⁂ *The Stage Is Set for Change* ⁂

Following the boom years of the 1920s, the waterfront stagnated and continued to decline through the Great Depression of the 1930s. The few changes that had been contemplated were further delayed by the outbreak of World War II. The waterfront had become derelict, dirty, and depressed. The once vibrant commercial boat activity was all but over. In December of 1931, the *Burlington Free Press* reported that for "the third consecutive year, not one dollar's worth of freight has come into Burlington by water from Canada and there is little likelihood that there ever will be any more."

As the waterfront's lumberyards failed, they were replaced by a blight of oil company storage tanks. The waterfront changes provoked a headline in a 1935 *Burlington Free Press* which observed that the "Lake Front Presents An Entirely Different Appearance From That of Years Ago, But Fire Hazard Remains to a Considerable Extent." By 1935, tanks along the waterfront stored 5,500,000 gallons of fuel.

Elisha Goodsell's homespun Burlington ferry operation finally went out of business, leaving his three formerly palatial yachts sunk in the harbor. Horace Corbin's plan to control and expand the lake's ferry traffic was devas-tated by World War II, and during the war he was barely able to keep his business afloat. By war's end, Corbin had sold his two streamline ferries, had cut up and sold *Chateaugay* and was in the process of selling *Vermont III*.

Aerial view of the Burlington Harbor, circa 1937. In this photograph taken by George Lathrop, the prewar Burlington waterfront has one of the Streamline Ferries loading cars just north of the College Street dock. At the end of the dock is the third yacht club with ferry advertisements on its roof. In the bottom and top of the picture are oil storage tanks. Railroad buildings are still present, but stacked lumber is no longer visible.
Courtesy Lake Champlain Transportation Company.

⊰ *After the War: A New Waterfront Perspective* ⊱

After the war, the public's perspective of the waterfront began to change. The Coast Guard had absorbed the Lighthouse Service and was planning to establish a permanent waterfront base. City officials were determined to clean up the waterfront; the old Lake Champlain Yacht Club was demolished and Goodsell's derelict boats were finally removed. Corbin purchased the car ferry *Mott Haven* and put it into service, but in 1948, with his health failing, he sold the ferry business to three young businessmen, Lewis Evans, Richard Wadhams and James Wolcott. These "Three Bears," as they became known, began investing in and invigorating the ferry service at Burlington, Charlotte, and Grand Isle.

The navy began planning for a Reserve Training Center at the foot of College Street on what had been the worst portion of the waterfront. The old Timothy Follett House was acquired by the Veterans of Foreign Wars for use as a new headquarters, and the numbers of recreational power boaters and marinas expanded rapidly. The city began to look upon its waterfront with a new and more appreciative eye and began to question its practice of dumping raw sewage into the harbor. On one occasion, in August of 1949, city firemen were tasked with spraying pine oil to combat the nauseating odor.

As appreciation for the waterfront grew, more public and private investments were finding their way to this part of the city. The U.S. Navy opened its reserve station and brought in *LSIL 799* to serve as their training ship. The city invested in its first sewage treatment plant and a lakefront beautification plan was begun. For the first time citizens and their governmental representatives looked at the

Steamboat Ticonderoga *begins its land journey to the Shelburne Museum, 1955.*
Photograph by McAllister of Burlington, courtesy Special Collections, Bailey/Howe Library, University of Vermont.

waterfront as a public resource. Acquisition of the Old Salt Dock as a new park and marina was proposed. This historic pier was successfully converted into a park and marina and was named for Dr. Charles Perkins who had championed the cause. Throughout this time the lake's last remaining operational steamboat, *Ticonderoga*, was struggling to survive, and in 1954 she finally left the lake for a permanent home at the newly-established Shelburne Museum.

But the evolution of the waterfront did not happen all at once, and the largely vacant waterfront became the home to a new junkyard and an electrical generating plant. Named for Mayor Moran, the coal fired plant sent so much soot and ash onto neighboring property that it was embroiled in controversy until operations finally ceased in 1986, when it was replaced by a wood-chip burning plant in a remote location in the city. The Navy's training ship proved to be too expensive for them to manage and so it was removed from the lake. However, the Coast Guard did successfully establish a permanent base on the site where Corbin had built his two Streamline Ferries.

The expanding road system and increasing use of automobiles and trucks impacted the railroads much as the railroads had crippled the steamboats. Passenger service through Burlington dropped to such low levels that it was finally abandoned. The old Union Station was sold to the Green Mountain Power Company and converted into office space. In 1964, the state took over the defunct Rutland Railroad's rights-of-way and leased them to the new Vermont Railway for freight operations. An attempt to restore limited passenger service from Burlington to Charlotte, Vermont, through the *Champlain Flyer*, begun in December of 2000, was suspended in 2003.

The issues that finally pushed the waterfront's future to center stage were the almost constant requests from oil companies to expand their capacity. By 1958, the Burlington waterfront had grown to eighty-three fuel holding tanks containing eighty-four million gallons of fuel. The fuel business did create a new period of revived lake commerce as 280 barges traveled from the Hudson River via the expanded New York State Barge Canal each year to supply the tank farms. The next fight for the future of the waterfront would focus on these tanks.

The Moran Electric Generating Plant, circa 1954.
From a private collection.

Tugboat Martin J. Kehoe *Pushing an Oil Barge on Lake Champlain, 1982.*
Photograph by the author.

95

Aerial View of Burlington, circa 1967. Urban renewal was in progress when this photograph was taken. Areas of demolition work can be seen in the lower left. Along the waterfront from left to right are the Pease Grain Company, Navy Reserve, Lake Champlain Transportation, Perkins Pier, fuel tanks, and the railroad.
From a private collection.

Tugboat **Wm. H. McAllister,** *Sunk in 1963, Lake Champlain.* While towing an empty gasoline barge, the tug ran up on Schuyler Reef. All hands escaped to the barge as the tugboat sank. This photograph was taken in 1997 with a remote-operated vehicle.
Photograph by Benthos Inc., from LCMM Collection.

LCTC Ferry Adirondack *Cruises North in Front of the Burlington Community Boathouse, 1994. Adirondack* was launched in 1913 as *South Jacksonville* and was powered by a coal-fired steam engine. *Adirondack* came to the lake in 1954 and is the longest serving double-ended American ferryboat of all time. The Burlington Community Boathouse was established in 1988. The second floor public function space is named in honor of James Wakefield, the hero of the *General Butler* sinking.
Photograph by the author.

A waterfront Friendship Fountain, which had aspirations of creating a permanent attraction in the form of an enormous column of water blowing skyward from the breakwater, was tried and failed. The possibility of an atomic-powered generating plant for the waterfront was discussed for many years. This proposal, to the relief of many, never emerged from the discussion phase. The Lake Champlain Transportation Company, (LCTC) began to adapt and expand their operations at the foot of historic King Street. The public debate had begun and harbor improvement lighted the way for more public access and activity. By the 1960s the issue of all those oil storage tanks was coming to a head. Support for the oil companies' interests was eroded by the almost constant oil slick soiling the harbor and by numerous barge accidents. The accidents continually reminded people that a catastrophic event could occur at almost anytime. After years of debate, a 1975 city ordinance finally gave the oil companies twenty years to vacate the waterfront.

The future was in sight. Burlington's waterfront, like waterfronts all over the country, was being rediscovered for its historic and aesthetic value and a number of development proposals were put forward. Government sponsored urban renewal cleared vast old waterfront neighborhoods and the Radisson hotel chain moved forward with plans for a 200-room facility on Battery Street overlooking the lake. While many old buildings of historical interest were lost to urban renewal, a number of the most historic lakefront buildings became the focus of restoration and adaptive reuse. The oil companies at first protested then later accepted their fate and began to dismantle their lakeshore facilities. The Pomerleau Agency purchased the Timothy Follett House and renovated it to its former glory. Momentum to create a public environment on the waterfront was increasing. A major step forward occurred when the City of Burlington challenged the railroads ownership of the extensive acreage that had been created by the dumping of fill into the lake in the second half of the nineteenth century. This breakthrough in the Public Trust Doctrine ultimately led to the city's purchase of much of the waterfront not in direct railroad use.

As the oil tanks began to disappear, a new sense of the waterfront emerged. As real estate developers came forward with dramatic new proposals for commercial waterfront development, city voters defeated most of them in favor of public use. A nine-mile bike path was established along the old railroad tracks and the City of Burlington brought a new Community Boathouse, designed to resemble the original yacht club building, to the former location of the old Lake Champlain Yacht Club. In the meantime, the historic Burlington Barge Canal was designated an EPA Superfund site, a process that was to take more than twenty years to resolve. Throughout this period, new businesses, restaurants, and retail stores were migrating closer to the former no-man's land; the renaissance had begun.

The large passenger schooners *Richard Robbins* and *Homer W. Dixon* each sailed from the waterfront for a few years and the excursion boats *Spirit of Ethan Allen I, II,* and now *III* have been rotating fixtures on the waterfront for more than two decades. In 2003, the LCTC's new excursion boat *Northern Lights,* was christened at the historic King Street Dock. The Union Station has become the Main Street Landing; the Burlington

ferries *Valcour, Champlain,* and *Adirondack* still carry on the proud tradition of lake crossing service. The Lake Champlain Community Sailing Center has taken over a portion of the former Moran Plant for community boating and four Underwater Shipwreck Preserves have been established in Burlington Harbor. A new waterfront sewage treatment plant promises to keep the beaches open and improve water quality and the U.S. Coast Guard Station Burlington, has a new modern facility. The venerable steamboat *Ticonderoga,* now on permanent display at the Shelburne Museum, has been completely restored with the support of Mac and Lois McClure. The University of Vermont built the new Rubenstein Ecosystem Laboratory and after forty-four years, the Navy Reserve Center left the waterfront and paved the way for the Lake Champlain Science Center, succeeded by ECHO at the Leahy Center for Lake Champlain. This new lake aquarium and science center is providing the public with a greater appreciation of the Champlain Basin ecosystem.

The Steamboat Ticonderoga, *1998.* After a six-year restoration project sponsored by Mac and Lois McClure and the estate of Ralph Nading Hill, the magnificent steamboat was re-christened.
Photograph by the author.

The Cruise Boat MV Northern Lights *Christened May 1, 2003.*
Photograph by Rick Norcross, courtesy Lake Champlain Cruises.

As many of the lake's historic lighthouses begin to be relit, the renaissance seems likely to continue. The waterfront of Gideon King and Timothy Follett has changed. Gone are the sleek sloops and schooners, the steamboats and canal boats that once dominated the seascape. The derelict vessels of the 1930s are gone. They have been replaced by a modern new fleet of excursion and recreational boats designed to satisfy the public's new interest in the history and the beauty of this very special place. As we approach the year 2009, the 400th Anniversary of Henry Hudson's and Samuel de Champlain's explorations, the waterfronts and the waterways of their namesakes, Lake Champlain and the Hudson River, shine with our new appreciation of their history and potential.

ECHO-Leahy Center for Lake Champlain, 2003.
Photograph by Greg Bessette, *St. Albans Messenger,* courtesy ECHO-Leahy Center.

Panorama, Burlington, Vermont, June 2002. In this photograph, the Burlington waterfront is captured as it appears today. From left to right, Waterfront Park and boardwalk, the Burlington Community Boathouse, the *Spirit of Ethan Allen III,* the ECHO-Leahy Center in-construction, the Lake Champlain Transportation Company facilities and Perkins Pier.
Photograph by Robert Lyons Photography.

Part IV

Rediscovering History

The Lake Champlain Maritime Museum's Research, Archaeology and Replica Programs

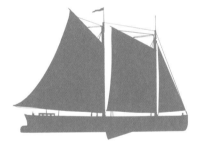

Building the Canal Schooner *Lois McClure*

The Skeleton of the Lois McClure, *June 2003.*
Photograph by Nick LaVecchia, LCMM Collection.

⚓ The Lake Champlain Maritime Museum ⚓

uring the past three decades the public's appreciation for Lake Champlain's cultural and ecological value has increased dramatically. The positive impact of these changing perceptions cannot be overstated. Recognition of the fragility of the lake's ecosystem led to the establishment of the Lake Champlain Basin Program, an initiative funded by the federal government, designed to bring together Vermont, New York, and Quebec, as well as U.S. and Canadian government representatives, to manage the diverse aspects of the Champlain Valley watershed. Along with public recognition of the lake and its connecting waterways' importance for recreation, as a source of drinking water, and as a dynamic fishery, there is a growing awareness of the lake's cultural heritage sites. Over the past decade, substantial restoration work and improvements in public access have taken place at the Mount Independence and Chimney Point historic sites in Vermont. These sites now join the better known forts at Ticonderoga and Crown Point, New York, in a network of popular cultural heritage sites located along the waterway from New York City to Montreal. The increasing interest in the maritime aspects of Lake Champlain's history and a growing recognition that the lake holds an extraordinary collection of intact historic shipwrecks, gave rise to a new museum.

The Lake Champlain Maritime Museum is dedicated to preserving and sharing the maritime history of the Lake Champlain region. Since the opening day in 1986, when the entire museum was housed in a historic stone schoolhouse saved from demolition and restored as the first exhibit building, the institution has grown to more than a dozen exhibit buildings reflecting on an ever widening body of information. The campus, which is located on land donated by the historic Basin Harbor Club, serves as the ideal venue for visitors to explore Lake Champlain's rich history.

(left)
Aboard the Philadelphia II, *circa 1995.*
LCMM Educators Erick Tichonuk (left) and Len Ruth (right) weave the story of Lake Champlain's Revolutionary War history for a group of students.
Photograph by Eric Bessette, LCMM Collection.

(right)
The Stone School House, 1986.
From the LCMM Collection.

(far right)
The Lake Champlain Maritime Museum During its Annual Small Boat Festival.
From the LCMM Collection.

The Colonial-era Bateau Perseverance, *1987.*
From the LCMM Collection.

One of the cornerstones of the LCMM's mission is to study Lake Champlain's extraordinary collection of historic shipwrecks and present that information to the public. A natural outgrowth of the LCMM's archaeological studies is the implementation of replica building projects. In the 1980s, the museum began the first of its experimental projects to construct full-sized working replicas of historic vessels as vehicles to teach the history and archaeology of Lake Champlain. The first replica boat, the Colonial-era bateau *Perseverance*, exceeded all expectations and convinced the museum that this was an effective process. In 1989, LCMM initiated a three-year effort to build a working replica of the Revolutionary War gunboat *Philadelphia*. With the rare endorsement of the Smithsonian Institution, which exhibits the original *Philadelphia*, the *Philadelphia II* was launched in 1991 to the cheers of more than four thousand people. The extraordinary success of that project to stimulate interest in this important national story convinced museum planners that a well-designed replica project had great power to teach history. Replica projects also serve as a cost-effective alternative to the expensive and often destructive process of raising historic shipwrecks. Now, the *Philadelphia II* is boarded every year by thousands of school children and visitors at the museum.

The Revolutionary War gunboat Philadelphia II *on her launching day, August 1991.*
From the LCMM Collection.

On board Philadelphia II, *1995.* Dale Henry with his back to the camera teaches the class.
From the LCMM Collection.

The Lake Champlain Underwater Preserve Program

One of the most challenging elements of underwater resource management is public access. Who gets access to these underwater sites? How do we protect the wooden ships from anchor damage? Will divers respect the shipwrecks as underwater museums? Can the shipwrecks be visited safely? How should such an underwater public access program be managed?

In 1985, *General Butler*, the steamboat *Phoenix*, which burned in 1819, and *A.R. Noyes*, a standard canal boat that sank in 1884, became the first sites within a new underwater preserve program administered by the Vermont Division for Historic Preservation. This was one of the first programs of its type in the country and has become a model for other jurisdictions. Today, the preserves have eight shipwreck sites that are seasonally buoyed to facilitate safe diver access. The moorings identify the locations of the shipwrecks and provide a place to secure the divers' boat, thereby eliminating the need for anchoring. Today, in Burlington Harbor, divers can not only visit *General Butler*, but can also explore the canal schooner *O.J. Walker*, and the only known intact archaeological example of a horse-powered ferryboat in the world.

The Author at the Phoenix *Underwater Preserve Buoy, 1985.*
From the LCMM Collection.

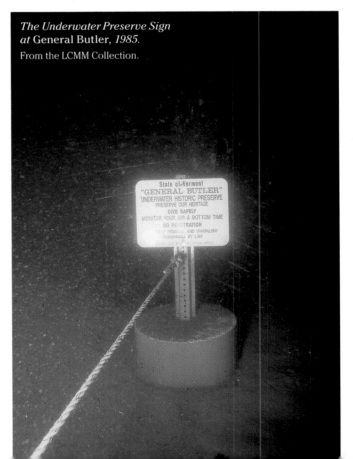

The Underwater Preserve Sign at **General Butler**, *1985.*
From the LCMM Collection.

Water Witch *with an LCMM Maritime Research Institute Diver Examining the Bow Assembly, 2002.*
Photograph by Pierre LaRocque, LCMM Collection.

Philadelphia II *in North Harbor, circa 1998.*
From the LCMM Collection.

Model Maker Win Lewis with a Model of Philadelphia, *2001.*
Photograph by Eric Bessette.

The Lake Champlain Maritime Museum's focus on the history and nautical archaeology of the Champlain Valley has been well received and resulted in the development of a permanent campus at historic Basin Harbor. The campus serves as an effective venue for visitors of all ages to discover and explore the body of history that helped define North America. The interaction of artifacts, images, film, and vessels weave a story about a sequence of history and a collection of shipwrecks that increases our understanding of events that forged a nation.

(above) *A Hard-hat Diving System Used by Col. Lorenzo Hagglund on Exhibit in the Nautical Archaeology Center.*

(below) *In the Revolutionary War Exhibit* Key to Liberty.
From the LCMM Collection.

Noah at the Wheel of the Merritime Play-ship.
Photograph by Eric Bessette.

The United States Coast Guard Buoy Tender 52302 Built in 1944.
From the LCMM Collection.

In the Blacksmith Shop.
From the LCMM Collection.

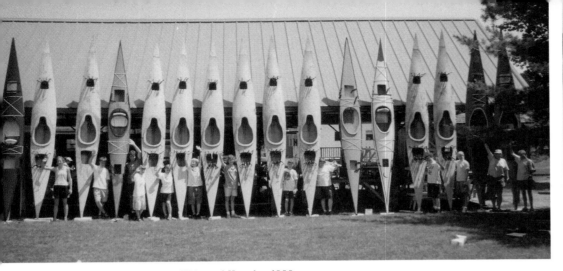

Champlain Discovery Kids and Kayaks, 1999.
From the LCMM Collection.

Champlain Longboat Red Wing *During the Spring Wave, 2001.*
From the LCMM Collection.

Today the Museum has grown and developed a mixture of programs designed to engage the public in a greater appreciation of place. Each season LCMM offers a Lecture Series covering a wide range of subjects. In 2003 the LCMM opened its new Hoehl Family Education and Visitors Center, providing a wonderful new auditorium to serve this expanding series. The Champlain Longboats and Champlain Discovery programs give young people an opportunity to build boats that they will use to explore Lake Champlain. They learn boat building skills, and in the process discover an important sense of themselves. The Paddling Ecology Program combines on-the-water activity with history and science. The annual Courses and Workshop programs provide a way to learn traditional woodworking and blacksmithing skills under the tutelage of experts. The Youth Programs offer entry into a similar world to children as young as three years old. The pounding of iron in the blacksmith shop, the ongoing artifact stabilization activity in the Conservation Laboratory, and the almost constant boat building in the Boat Shop all help increase public appreciation for Lake Champlain.

The Hoehl Education and Visitors Center Which Opened in 2003.
From the LCMM Collection.

Paddling Ecology 2001.
From the LCMM Collection.

The Maritime Research Institute

Below the waters of Lake Champlain rest archaeological sites from each of the region's historical eras. The lake's wrecks, in particular, represent one of the best-preserved collections of wooden shipwrecks in North America. Through the study of how they were built, the artifacts found on board, and the cargos they carried, these complex sites provide a window into past cultures and events.

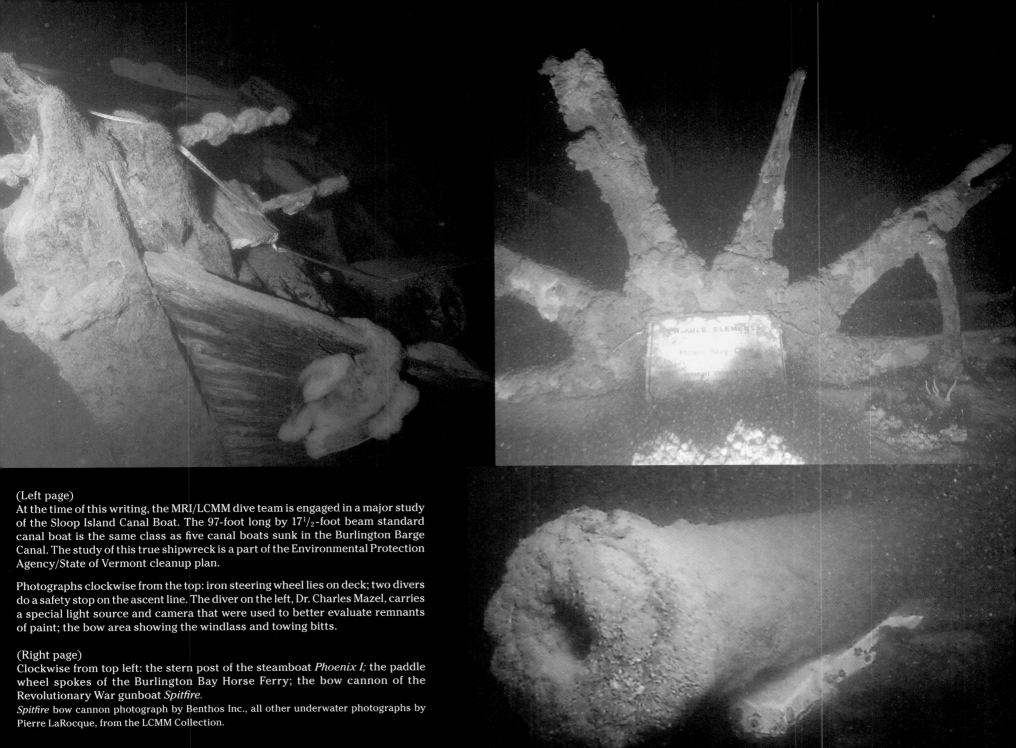

(Left page)
At the time of this writing, the MRI/LCMM dive team is engaged in a major study of the Sloop Island Canal Boat. The 97-foot long by $17^1/_2$-foot beam standard canal boat is the same class as five canal boats sunk in the Burlington Barge Canal. The study of this true shipwreck is a part of the Environmental Protection Agency/State of Vermont cleanup plan.

Photographs clockwise from the top: iron steering wheel lies on deck; two divers do a safety stop on the ascent line. The diver on the left, Dr. Charles Mazel, carries a special light source and camera that were used to better evaluate remnants of paint; the bow area showing the windlass and towing bits.

(Right page)
Clockwise from top left: the stern post of the steamboat *Phoenix I*; the paddle wheel spokes of the Burlington Bay Horse Ferry; the bow cannon of the Revolutionary War gunboat *Spitfire*.
Spitfire bow cannon photograph by Benthos Inc., all other underwater photographs by Pierre LaRocque, from the LCMM Collection.

Recovery of the Splintered Cannon from the Gunboat New York. The cannon was located by Ed Scollon in 1999 and recovered in 2001. The discovery stimulated the multiyear Valcour Bay Research Project, the systematic mapping of the Valcour Island submerged battlefield.
Photograph by Eric Bessette, from the LCMM Collection.

Conservation Lab Technician Sarah Lyman Working on a Bayonet Recovered from Valcour Island.
From the LCMM Collection.

The systematic study of the lake's shipwrecks was begun in 1980 by the Champlain Maritime Society. This group studied the canal schooner *General Butler,* the steamboat *Phoenix,* the War of 1812 brig *Eagle,* and the British sloop *Boscawen,* among others. The wealth of information generated by this work led to the founding of the Lake Champlain Maritime Museum (LCMM) in 1986. The common purpose of these institutions was a desire to study Lake Champlain's shipwrecks and share that information with the public.

In the 1990s the LCMM continued its research and preservation activities through the study of sites such as the Burlington Bay Horse Ferry, the steamboat *Champlain II,* the canal schooner *O.J. Walker,* and two War of 1812 wrecks near Whitehall, New York. Many of these studies were undertaken as joint efforts with the University of Vermont and the Institute of Nautical Archaeology at Texas A&M University. All of these efforts resulted in technical reports as well as in exhibits and displays for public enjoyment and education.

In 1997, LCMM opened an archaeological conservation laboratory, a critical step in the organization's goal of preserving material recovered from Lake Champlain. The conservation laboratory, in addition to treating artifacts from LCMM's research, also serves as a resource to help other institutions stabilize and preserve their archaeological collections.

(below)
A Photo Mosaic of Standard Canal Boat. One of five 97-foot class sunk in the Burlington Barge Canal that was made visible during a partial draining of the barge canal in a winter 2003 cleanup.
Photo mosaic by Chris Sabick and Adam Kane, from the LCMM Collection.

Lake Champlain Maritime Museum's most ambitious archaeological study to date is the Lake Survey Project, a systematic survey of all of Lake Champlain using side scan sonar. The Lake Survey was spurred on by the 1993 discovery of zebra mussels in Lake Champlain. These non-native, aquatic nuisance species encrust the wrecks, making their documentation extremely difficult and creating a microenvironment that speeds their decay. In 1996, the Lake Champlain Basin Program authorized LCMM to implement a lakewide survey to inventory all cultural resources in Lake Champlain. In the Lake Survey done between 1996 and 2003, over one hundred shipwrecks were located. The Survey's final product will be a comprehensive management plan, which will make recommendations for the preservation, protection, and interpretation of Lake Champlain's underwater archaeological sites.

In 2000, the dynamic and expanding nature of the LCMM's archaeological research activities prompted the formation of the Maritime Research Institute (MRI). The MRI, essentially the research arm of the LCMM, has had a very busy first few years. Two ambitious archaeological data recovery projects have been implemented: one on four scow barges in Alburg, Vermont, and a second on a standard canal boat in Charlotte, Vermont. In addition, the MRI has orchestrated the Valcour Bay Research Project, a systematic survey of the Revolutionary War battlefield scatter left from the Battle of Valcour Island in 1776.

In the future, the MRI plans to continue the study of the lake's shipwrecks begun over 20 years ago. As a result of these years of dedicated study, we now have an excellent grasp of most of what is on the bottom of Lake Champlain, and the MRI staff feels privileged to study, preserve, and interpret this vast collection of archaeological resources for the public.

Standard Canal Boat Emerges During Barge Canal Draining, 2002.
From the LCMM Collection.

The Revolutionary War Gunboat Spitfire, *1997.*
Painting by Ernie Haas, from the LCMM Collection.

An Old Timer on Lake Champlain. This circa 1900 postcard shows the 1862-class canal schooner *P.E. Havens,* built at Essex, New York, in 1865. From the LCMM Collection.

An Old Timer on Lake Champlain

⊰ *The Archaeology of the Lake Champlain Sailing Canal Boat* ⊱

I n 1980, two young divers discovered a shipwreck on the southwest end of the Burlington Breakwater and triggered the rediscovery of a forgotten class of North American naval architecture. The discovery of *General Butler* became the catalyst for a new research effort to put these working freight carriers into a perspective of their time. Since that initial study, MRI has also completed the documentation of *O.J. Walker,* another 1862-class canal schooner, coincidently also sunk within Burlington Harbor. A preliminary study of the Isle La Motte shipwreck has provided information about the 1841-class canal sloops and the recent discovery during the Lake Survey of the canal schooner *Troy* of Westport has provided us with the first, and currently the only, archaeological information about the original 1823-class vessels. The 1873-class canal schooner, the final step in the evolution of the sailing canal boat, has yet to yield an archaeological example. The information presented here provides a summary of these studies to date and the archaeological background for the Burlington Schooner Project, the current effort to build, launch and sail a full-sized working replica of an 1862-class canal schooner.

LCMM's research team has benefitted from contributions by a number of talented underwater photographers. Unless otherwise credited, the underwater photographs in this section were taken by Russ Bellico, John Butler, Joseph Cozzi, Leslie Lange, Pierre LaRocque, Dave Robinson and the author.

Bow of Canal Schooner O.J. Walker, *1996.*
From the LCMM Collection.

A Diver Records the Marble Blocks Inside General Butler, *1996.*
From the LCMM Collection.

The Wreck of Troy of Westport, An 1823-class Canal Schooner

In 1825, the canal schooner *Troy* disappeared off Westport, New York, during a November gale, taking five young men and boys to their death. The loss of *Troy* has remained one of Lake Champlain's greatest tragedies and mysteries. 175 years after its loss, LCMM's Lake Survey Project discovered the vessel in the lake's cold, deep waters.

Troy was sailing to Westport with a load of iron ore for the newly established Westport iron furnace. The schooner, under the command of twenty-five year old Captain Jacob Halstead, was carrying the captain's thirteen-year old brother, George, his half brother Jacob Pardee, and two crewmen, Daniel Cannon and John Williams. All were lost in the sinking.

Back on shore, the boys' mother and sisters [were] sitting at home... listening through the storm for the sound of homecoming footsteps as the night wore on. Suddenly they heard the boys on the doorsteps, stomping off the snow in the entry as they were wont to do before coming in. The women sprang to the door and opened it, stepped to the outer door and looked down upon the light carpet of untrodden snow which lay before it, and then crept trembling back to the fireside, knowing that sons and brothers would never sit with them again in its firelight.
—From *A History of Westport, Essex Co., New York*, by Carolyn Halstead Royce

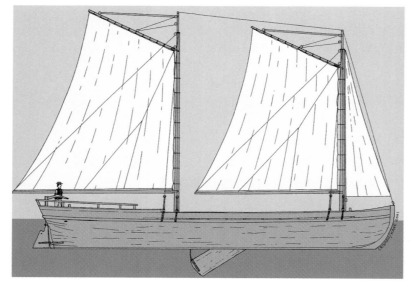

Conjectural Drawing of Troy *Under Sail.*
Drawn by Kevin Crisman and Adam Kane, from the LCMM Collection.

Memorial Marker. In the Westport Cemetery to the captain and crew of the schooner *Troy* of Westport.
Photograph by Peter Barranco, Jr., from the LCMM Collection.

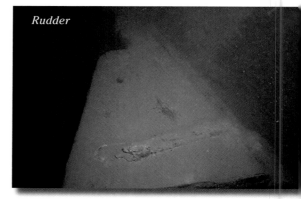

Rudder

Deadeye

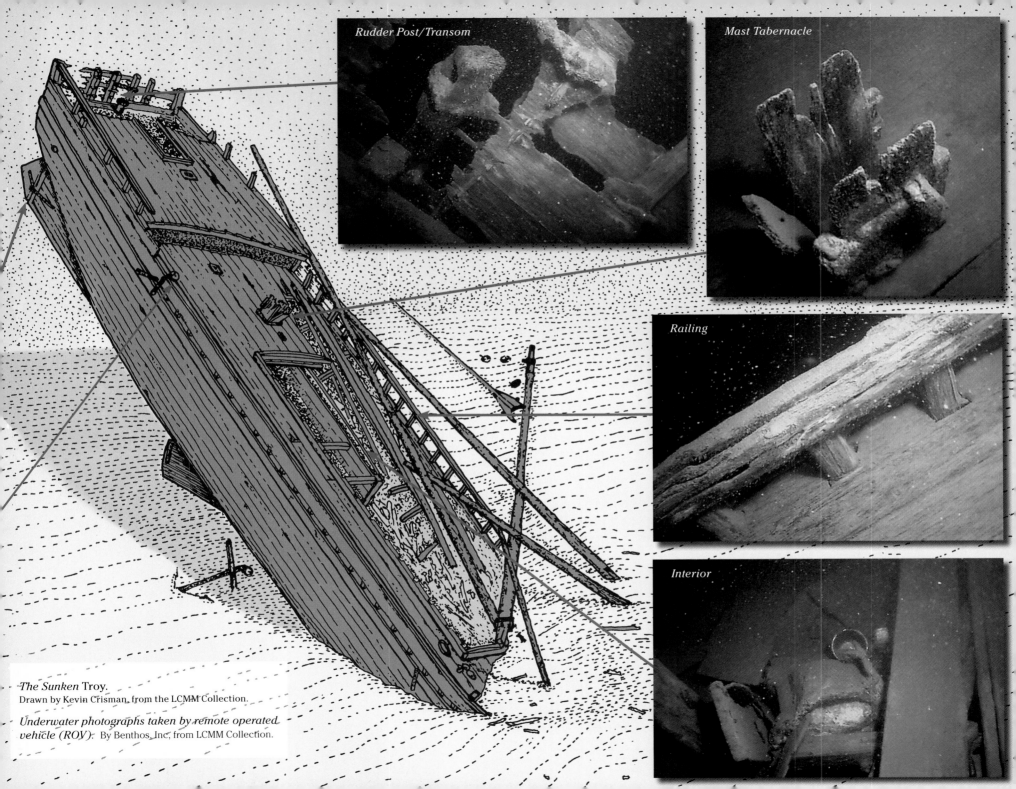

Rudder Post/Transom

Mast Tabernacle

Railing

Interior

The Sunken Troy.
Drawn by Kevin Crisman, from the LCMM Collection.

Underwater photographs taken by remote operated vehicle (ROV). By Benthos, Inc, from LCMM Collection.

The Isle La Motte Shipwreck, An 1841-class Canal Sloop

Often, when a shipwreck is discovered and its name, origin or the circumstances of its sinking are unknown, it is named for some other convenient reference. This was the case with the shipwreck located in 1978 by a group of Canadian archaeologists searching for a War of 1812 vessel reputed to be lost in the waters around Isle La Motte. It was believed the vessel sank during its retreat from the September 1814 Battle of Plattsburgh Bay. The renowned Dr. Harold Edgerton of M.I.T. was the survey's sonar operator and two promising targets were located. The following season the group, the Committee of Underwater Archaeology and History of Quebec, returned to investigate their two sonar targets. The most promising 1812 shipwreck target proved to be a geological feature and not a shipwreck, but the second target was determined to be a mid-nineteenth century commercial craft, dubbed the "Isle La Motte shipwreck."

The Isle La Motte wreck is a representative of the 1841-class canal sloop, making her dimensions 79 feet long and 13½ feet in beam, with a depth of hold between four and five feet. A preliminary examination of the hull determined that she was carrying a cargo of stone when she sank, that her stern cabin roof had lifted off during the sinking and that she was steered by a tiller rather than a wheel. She lies slightly down at the bow, with a starboard list, in soft sediment. Her single mast is missing but the distinctive, three-sided mast tabernacle and the iron collar that secured the mast is present. The Isle La Motte wreck and one other shipwreck, recently located during LCMM's Lake Survey, are the only intact examples of the 1841-class of canal sloops.

Research uncovered by LCMM historian Peter Barranco may have located the circumstances of the Isle La Motte canal boat's loss, although the vessel's name still remains a mystery. The September 5, 1846, *Plattsburgh Republican* newspaper reported:

Accident.–Mr. Daniel Hall, an industrious citizen of this town, who was employed in carrying stone on a small sloop from Gilman's quary [sic] to the new Fort at Rouse's Point, was drowned on the night of the 2nd. Inst. When within a few miles of Rouse's Point a sudden squall struck his vessel, which was heavily laden, and in endeavoring to throw the anchor over he was caught by the cable, the vessel partly capsized, filled and sunk-taking him down with it. His son and another man who were on board saved themselves with much difficulty.

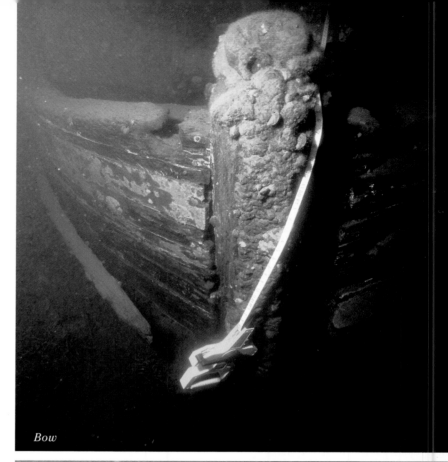

Bow

Deadeye

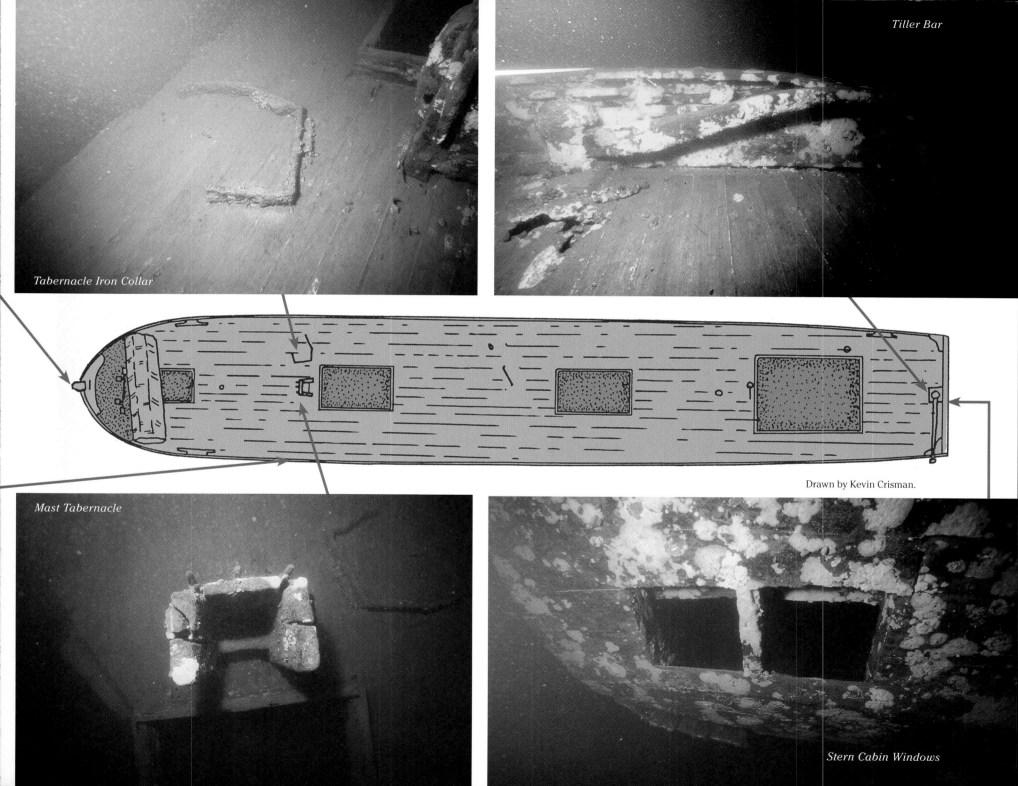

Tabernacle Iron Collar

Tiller Bar

Mast Tabernacle

Drawn by Kevin Crisman.

Stern Cabin Windows

⊰ General Butler, *An 1862-Class Canal Schooner* ⊱

One of the best documented shipwrecks in Lake Champlain is the 1862-class canal schooner *General Butler.* The boat was named after a Massachusetts lawyer who became a general, and a hero during the early months of the Civil War. Vermonters Jabez Rockwell and Edwin Langdon, who had commissioned the boat at the well-established Essex, New York, shipyard of Hoskins and Ross, presumably named the vessel as a patriotic gesture. *General Butler* began service in 1862, and by the time of her sinking had had three different owners: Rockwell and Langdon sold the boat to Julius Rugar of Plattsburgh, New York, and he in turn, sold to William Montgomery of Isle La Motte, Vermont.

William Montgomery was captain of *General Butler* on Saturday, December 9, 1876, when heavy winter gales drove the vessel toward the north end of the Burlington Breakwater. *General Butler* carried a load of Isle La Motte marble for delivery to the Burlington Marble Works; also on board were one deck hand, Montgomery's teenaged daughter Cora and a schoolgirl friend, and Elisha Goodsell, a quarry operator from Isle La Motte. The girls planned some Christmas shopping in Burlington; Goodsell traveled to get medical treatment for an eye injury. The power of the storm was too much for the steering mechanism of the aging *General Butler,* and just off the breakwater, according to press accounts, "the vessel began to drift at the mercy of the wind and waves."

The plight of Captain Montgomery and *General*

Village of Essex, New York, 1846. Burlington was not the only community to benefit from commerce on the lake. Essex, New York emerged as a commercial and boat building port in the early part of the nineteenth century. Home to one of the lake's most active shipyards, *General Butler* was built here in 1862.
From a private collection.

William Montgomery on the stern of the schooner J.P. Howard, circa 1880.
Courtesy Isle La Motte Historical Society.

Butler suggests the economic need that drove commercial sailors to dare winter's worst for one last cargo. Intrepid captains risked cold water, freezing temperatures, and frostbite to earn a little more money before shipping was halted for the winter. The passenger list suggests Montgomery expected a routine delivery. Sailors in 1876 had no radar, weather forecasting, or radio communications. They relied on their experience in scanning the sky to predict the weather. In this case, Montgomery miscalculated.

As *General Butler* drifted southward, the deck hand threw over the storm anchor in a vain attempt to keep the vessel from crashing into the breakwater's stone-filled cribs. Meanwhile, Captain Montgomery attempted to rig a spare tiller bar onto the ship's steering gear. With the tiller bar chained in place, Montgomery ordered the anchor line severed with an axe, and he attempted to round the

General Butler *Striking the Burlington Breakwater December 9, 1876.* Drawing by Kevin Crisman, from LCMM Collection.

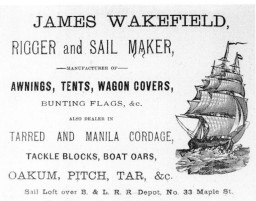

James Wakefield Rigger and Sail Maker. From *Gazetteer and Business Directory of Chittenden County, Vermont.* 1882.

James Wakefield, circa 1900. Courtesy Special Collections, Bailey/Howe Library, University of Vermont.

southern end of the breakwater. He did not make it. A short distance from the southern lighthouse, *General Butler* smashed into the breakwater. The passengers, crew, and captain were able to leap to the frozen haven of the breakwater. Captain Montgomery was the last to leave the ship. Immediately after he jumped at the crest of a large wave, *General Butler* sank in forty feet of water, its stone cargo propelling it downward. Stranded on the open breakwater, whipped by fierce winds and driving snow, and soaked by heavy waves, the refugees from *General Butler* might have died had it not been for James Wakefield and his son, Jack.

Although dozens of lakemen had flocked to the wharves in response to *General Butler's* plight, only the Wakefields acted. They seized a small government lighthouse boat and rowed out to the breakwater. Captain Montgomery lifted his daughter and her young friend into James Wakefield's arms, and as scores of people watched from the shore, the groggy Goodsell, the deck hand, and finally Montgomery clambered into the bobbing rescue craft. Wakefield and his son rowed them safely to shore.

Bystanders took the chilled survivors to J. Sullivan's house on Battery Street where Dr. H.H. Langdon examined them. Shortly, all were pronounced out of danger. The *Burlington Free Press* commented on December 12, "It was Miss Montgomery's first trip in her father's boat, and she showed a goodly degree of Yankee grit, for the first question she asked on returning to consciousness was that she might be allowed to make the return trip when the schooner would be raised." Although the masts, rigging, and some other equipment were recovered, the hull of *General Butler* never was. Today, the remains of the schooner still rest in forty feet of water off Burlington's breakwater.

Cora Montgomery, circa 1878. Courtesy Isle La Motte Historical Society.

119

General Butler *Today*

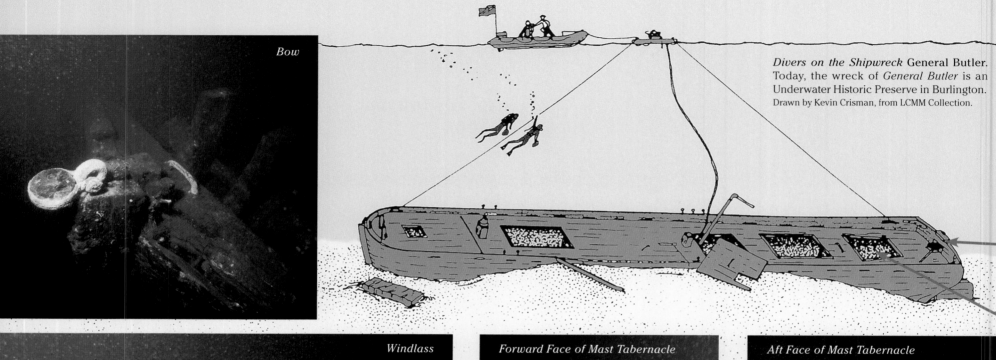

Divers on the Shipwreck General Butler. Today, the wreck of *General Butler* is an Underwater Historic Preserve in Burlington. Drawn by Kevin Crisman, from LCMM Collection.

Bow

Windlass

Forward Face of Mast Tabernacle

Aft Face of Mast Tabernacle

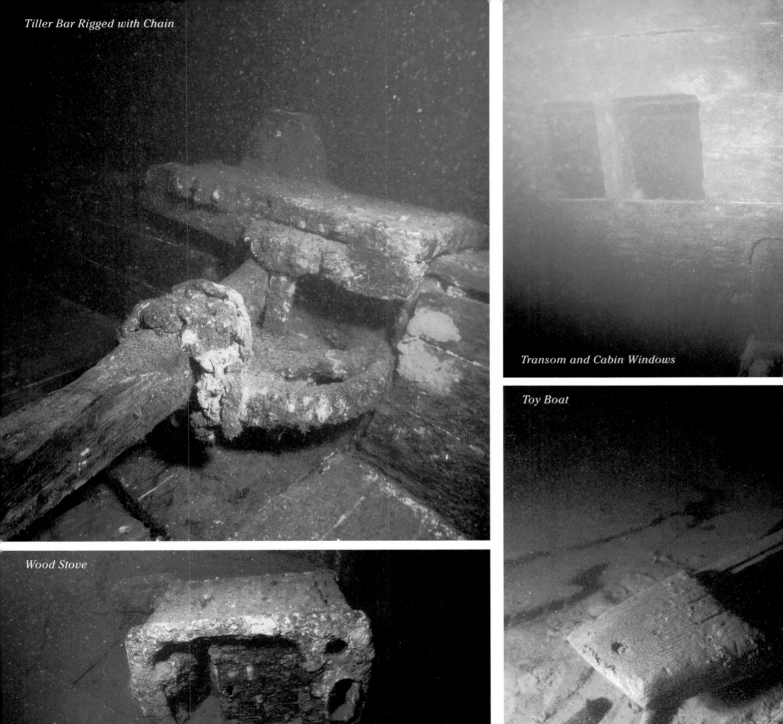

Tiller Bar Rigged with Chain

Transom and Cabin Windows

Toy Boat

Wood Stove

Canal Schooner at the Shelburne Dock of William Seward Webb, circa 1895.
Courtesy Shelburne Farms.

⛵ O.J. Walker, *An 1862-class Canal Schooner* ⛵

O.J. *Walker* was launched into Burlington Harbor by shipwright Orson Saxton Spear in 1862, and after an extraordinarily long career, she sank here thirty-three years later. The new schooner's first owner was Joseph Kirby of Burlington, who named the vessel for respected merchant Obadiah Johnson Walker. O.J. *Walker* had many owners, and during her long years of service, freighted lumber, coal, iron ore, farm products, stone, and many other Champlain Valley products. Once, in 1882, she was actually hired as a pleasure boat for a chaperoned group of teenagers sailing to St. John's (St. Jean), Quebec. Her last owners were John W. and Henry Brown, father and son, who operated a large brick and tile works in Malletts Bay, with a sales yard in Burlington.

Obadiah J. Walker 1828–1897.
From LCMM Collection.

O.J. Walker & Brothers Wholesale Grocers.
From *Gazetteer and Business Directory of Chittenden County, Vermont,* 1882.

On her last voyage, *O. J. Walker* carried a load of brick and tile for the Shelburne estate of Dr. William Seward Webb. It was May 11, 1895, and the thirty-three year old boat encountered a severe wind storm.

> *Those who were on shore in a position to see the storm-swept lake, uninfluenced by considerations of personal security, pronounced the scene magnificent in its wildness, and old Champlain is seldom disturbed as it was then. Considerations of an entirely different nature occupied the minds of those who were out in boats and subjected to the violence of the elements.*
>
> —*Essex County Republican,* May 16, 1895.

O. J. Walker was indeed "subjected to the violence of the elements." To make matters worse, her crew had loaded the cargo not in the hold, but on the deck. Loading the cargo on the deck would have saved time on both ends of the trip, but would have been much more stressful on the schooner's old hull. Unfortunately, the severity of the storm and the position of the cargo caused the old boat to spring a leak. The captain, W. J. Worthen, had just enough time to drop an anchor and get his wife and crewman into a small boat. As *O. J. Walker* turned on her side, most of her cargo was dumped to the lake bottom. The vessel momentarily righted herself, but filled with water. *O. J. Walker* sank to the lake bottom in about 65 feet of water. Captain Worthen and his crew were without oars, but were blown safely to shore.

Trade Card for John W. and Henry W. Brown Brick and Tile at Mallets Bay and Burlington.
From an ad in the *Burlington Free Press.*

⚓ O.J. Walker *Today* ⚓

Mast Tabernacle

Diver Examines the Top of the Centerboard at the Deck

Bow

Bricks

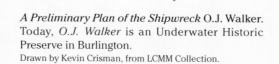

A Preliminary Plan of the Shipwreck O.J. Walker.
Today, *O.J. Walker* is an Underwater Historic
Preserve in Burlington.
Drawn by Kevin Crisman, from LCMM Collection.

Tile by Stern Cabin

Main Mast Trestle Tree

Hand Truck on Tile and Brick

Ship's Wheel

Canal Boats in Tow, circa 1890. A tow of canal boats at least four across.
Photograph by Howard Pyle, courtesy Fort Ticonderoga Museum.

⊰ Life on Board a Canal Boat ⊱

When the wreck of *General Butler* was discovered in 1980, the fascinating history of Lake Champlain's sailing canal boats had been all but forgotten. The discovery prompted new research, which over the past two decades has uncovered priceless new information about these watercraft, and the people who built, sailed, and lived aboard them. New shipwreck discoveries in the past few years have continued to provide more information on these unique vessels. The Lake Champlain Maritime Museum, using all manner of research to better understand the maritime history of the region has recently identified two new sources of information. The personal recollections of Cora Archambault and the journals of Theodore Bartley demonstrate the building-block nature of history, in which each new source adds to our knowledge base. Their commentaries have greatly enriched our understanding of the canal boat community.

⊰ Cora Archambault ⊱

Cora Archambault was born in 1904 to a canal boat family. Cora's father owned two standard canal boats and she spent her early years traveling the region's inland waterways during the eight-month canal season with her father, mother, brother and two sisters. Through Cora's personal recollections we see what life was like for a canal boat family during the first quarter of the twentieth century, and through her eyes we can see the cabin living arrangements and how daily routines were adapted aboard these freight boats.

All family life took place in their cabin in the canal boat's stern. The cabin had a roof above the deck level, with windows on the sides to let in light and air. Steep stairs descended to the cabin from a companionway in the port side aft corner of the cabin roof. The family's food was stored in a cupboard with sliding doors and deep shelves just to the side of the stairs, and the "cook room," or galley, was partitioned off from the rest of the cabin. The sleeping quarters were at the forward end of the cabin, with one bunk under the deck forward of the food cupboard. Cora and her younger sister Viola slept in that bunk; the other bed along the opposite wall "where my mother and father [slept;] that was their side."

Cora Archambault as a Teenager Living on Her Family's Canal Boats, circa 1918.
Courtesy of Cora Archambault.

Cora Archambault Outside Her Home at the Fiddlers Elbow, Whitehall, New York, 2000.
Photograph by the author, from the LCMM Collection.

The Cabin of the Erie Canal Boat Rose *in 1954.*
Courtesy Canal Society of New York State.

*Lake Champlain Steam Towboats and Canal Boats in
Winter Quarters at Whitehall, New York, circa 1900.*
Courtesy Canal Society of New York State.

The parent's bed was curtained off from the rest of the cabin interior. Cora's older brother and sister slept on the family's other boat. There was a drop leaf table in the middle of the cabin with six chairs, and over the table hung a lamp that swayed with the movement of the boat. Cora's family had one rocking chair and "my mother had a sewing machine and she could sing canal songs in French and English." The cabin floors were covered with linoleum and throw rugs; the windows had curtains and there were also a few plants. A galvanized tub for bathing was stored on the cabin roof when not in use. "It was very neat, very comfortable, very homelike."

The family even had pets on the boat. They were given rabbits by a farm family from along the Champlain Canal at Northumberland, and they had a cat named Theodore that used to walk with them along the towpath. They carried a barrel of fresh water up at the bow. "When we got to Lake Champlain, way out the water was beautiful and clear, and they would send back word, 'Don't anybody empty your slop buckets or throw anything in the water because we're going to fill the water barrels,' they filled the fixed barrels with buckets lowered over the side."

"We used to love to go to New York. Father would set up the wheelhouse forward of the cabin and just aft of the cargo hatches. All the tows that would go down the river and come back, there was a little boat…and they would carry vegetables and all sorts of goodies on it. And it had a whistle that was very different from any whistle I ever heard. Why we would go down about Newburgh and we'd be looking for that bum boat…the tow would still go and he'd tie [up] to the outside boat. And the women used to wear big aprons and they'd go buy a lot of vegetables and fruit and they would fill their aprons. But what was best of all was the ice cream and that was a treat…"

Cora remembers that "there were a lot of families on these boats." Cora's family didn't stay on the boat year round, "My father could have done that. He could have worked the harbor in New York. But he didn't want to, and my mother didn't want him to. We had a home [here] in Whitehall over across the tracks. A pretty good-sized house… and so my father did carpenter work in the winter after the canal closed." After Cora's father retired from the canal, "Every spring he would get the fever. He'd get that ache to go on the boat." After he retired, he built himself a houseboat out of materials recycled from canal boats abandoned in the old channel so he could continue to get out on the water.

For more than a decade Cora grew up aboard the family's canal boats playing with her siblings in the cabin and on deck, always under the watchful eye of her parents, lest one of the children should fall into the water. Her mother would be downstairs and call up through the companionway, "Are you sitting [on top of the cabin]?" Cora's father was involved in a number of rescues of people who fell in the water. He saved a drunken man who fell in near their boat at Port Henry and "another time my father saved this little boy…sometimes there were quite good-sized families on boats. And this one little boy, he must have been four or five years old, and he was jumping from one

The Three Archambault Sisters, circa 1920. From left to right, Stella, Cora and Viola. Sister Stella was born on the family's canal boat.
Courtesy Cora Archambault.

Frank Archambault, at About Age 21, circa 1890. "He was never a big man. He never weighed more than 127 pounds, but he was like a cat. He was active…very quiet with a dry sense of humor… When my father was 15 years old, he was chewing tobacco and driving mules along the towpath."
Courtesy Cora Archambault.

Boy Overboard, 1860.
From an article in *Harper's New Monthly Magazine* 21 (122).

W.B. Fonda, *Loading Hay at Potash Point, circa 1890.*
Photograph by Howard Pyle, courtesy of the Fort Ticonderoga Museum.

boat to the other. Jumping back and forth and sometimes the boats would be close together and sometime they would swing far apart. My father got awful nervous. He said that little kid is certainly going to fall between those boats…finally it happened. The little fellow fell…down between the two boats. The men stood around and the women just stood screaming and nobody did anything. So my father said, 'I can't stand this' and he ran, and I remember my mother saying 'be careful now' and he tied this rope around his waist and he ran, and gave one end to someone and went down between the boats and got him out."

Cora has recounted another such incident, which occurred one day as the Archambault boats were tied up to a boom at Sorel, Quebec, at the junction of the Richelieu and the St. Lawrence Rivers. In this case it was Cora's younger sister Viola who needed to be rescued.

"Whenever we got to a place where we could go ashore, my mother used to put us ashore so that we could get exercise because we sat so much in the boat, and she figured we needed the exercise. And this place at Sorel there was a high bank there, but there were these booms. And between these booms and land was quite a stretch of water and it was deep there. Well, we had a load of hay on real high. So my mother told my brother to go around with the rowboat to the end of the boom and pick us up and bring us ashore. So my older sister, she was about 12, [mother] told her to watch us 'til we'd got in the boat, and my brother would take us over to the shore. Well, she was careless…and my [younger] sister, she was four years old, instead of making her stand on to the side of the ladder, she stepped backwards and went into the water…and we all stood there screaming. And my father was taking a nap. He must have been up all night for some reason or other. My mother, she heard us scream and she came down and she got halfway down the ladder and saw what happened. She couldn't swim, but she jumped in the water. She got my sister by the hand, but she was holding her underwater. And I remember holding my mother's arm…but she couldn't keep herself up and keep my sister's head above water. So my father heard us screaming and he was way up on this big high load of hay and he come and in one glance he saw what was

130

happening. And he dove off of that load of hay right into the water. And in no time he had both my mother and sister out. Well, they got the doctor for my sister, to roll her and see if she had water in her lungs. But she was all right. The only thing that upset her was that she lost one of her new pair of patent leather slippers—she lost one of those in the water. And that was the only worst thing that happened to her." Cora later recalled, "I always said my father was an unsung hero."

Cora's father had hauled pulpwood, lumber, sand, fertilizer, iron ore, coal, ice, grain, bags of sugar, and hay between New York City and Montreal on the Hudson River, Champlain Canal, Lake Champlain, Richelieu River/Chambly Canal and St. Lawrence waterways, frequently called the Northern or Champlain Waterway. Finally, the diminishing opportunities in the changing transportation system forced Frank Archambault to give up the tiller and retire to dry land. Cora's family moved to the Fiddler's Elbow at the northern entrance to the old channel leading to Whitehall, New York, taking up residence on the grounds of the now quiet Henry Neddo shipyard. Cora began her observations of everyday life on the canal system at the beginning of the twentieth century. By this time the sailing canal boats had all disappeared from the waterways, earlier victims of changing times and the evolution of transportation technology. By Cora's time the commercial boatman's niche had narrowed and it was now cost-effective to move only large numbers of standard canal boats through the lake or river under the power of a large steam tug.

Frank Archambeault with his Boat the W.S. Slingsby, *circa 1920.*
Courtesy of Cora Archambeault.

A Canal Tow, circa 1890.
Photograph by Howard Pyle, courtesy of
the Fort Ticonderoga Museum.

Sunday on the Canal, 1873.
From *Harper's Weekly.* October 18, 1873.

⊰ *Theodore Bartley* ⊱

John Henry Chubb and Eva Chubb, circa 1860.
Courtesy Barbara Bartley.

Theodore and Mary Bartley, circa 1863.
Courtesy Barbara Bartley.

Captain Theodore Bartley, circa 1865.
Courtesy Barbara Bartley.

Small Boats at Dresden, New York, circa 1865.
Courtesy Barbara Bartley.

The recent discovery of almost thirty years of journals recorded by Captain Theodore Bartley from 1861 to 1889 provides perhaps the best insight into the daily life of a canal boat captain, the operation of a sailing canal vessel, and the changing times that finally led to their operational demise.

Theodore Bartley grew up near Lake Erie and at age twenty-one left home and shipped out from New Bedford, Massachusetts, on the whaling ship *California*. After four years at sea, Theodore returned home to Norwalk, Ohio, to pursue his trade as a gunsmith and there he married Mary Felton. When Theodore's sister, Evalina, died unexpectedly, his life's course took an uncharted turn to the community of Dresden, New York, on the shore of Lake Champlain's southern narrows. His sister had been married to John Henry Chubb, who along with several brothers and extended family made their living on the Northern Waterway. When Evalina died, Theodore and Mary moved to Dresden to become surrogate parents for her children.

Theodore, already an accomplished mariner, became partners in a new canal boat with his brother-in-law John Henry and began a new career navigating along the Northern Waterways. They even occasionally hauled freight out to Buffalo, New York, and other destinations along the Erie Canal and other of the interconnecting New York State canals. Their new boat was christened the *Mary Eva* for Theodore's wife and his recently departed sister. Theodore records in his journal on April 24, 1861, that "yesterday Henry Chubb & Myself signed articles with Mr. [John] Adams agreeing to pay $1742 [$33,722 in 2000 dollars] for a lake canal boat built by them. Henry having already paid $100 down in money, we are to pay $50 per month with interest up to time of [final] payment." The sailing canal boat became Theodore and Mary's family home for the next decade. Theodore's journal entries describe the routes he traveled, the loads he carried, the almost constant repairs he made, the endless loading

Towing Receipt from the Steamboat George Washington, *1866.*
Courtesy Barbara Bartley.

and unloading, the uncertain search for the next freight, and the frustrations of waiting for the right wind when attempting to sail.

Through Theodore's journals we learn that deck loads, in addition to a load in the cargo hold, seemed to be a quite common way to maximize the value of the trip, even though it had to be lightered off before they could enter the canal and reloaded once they left the canal. On one dramatic trip in November 1861, Theodore and Mary were returning from Canada with a load of oats both in the cargo hold and in bins built above deck. On this particular journey, they had left St. Jean, with the wind behind them, being towed with other canal boats by the steam towboat *Ethan Allen.* When they arrived in the vicinity of Cumberland Head, the wind shifted and began to blow hard from the south.

Theodore's journal records the near disaster "when we began to round the head [Cumberland] all the boats began to strike heavily together. We broke between Adam [Chubb] & our boat [a] fender three inches thick and one foot wide. At one crush we began to roll quite heavily from the deck load being top heavy. Our boat would lay over to port quite heavy and hang there every time before righting finally. Just as we began to turn

the point of the breakwater at Plattsburg[h] she rolled heavy to starboard when Adam [Chubb] Henry [Chubb] & Myself all watched to see if she would right but found soon that she must either capsize entirely or throw off her deck load then right. I ran to tell Mary and Cinda [Felton] to leave the cabin but found they already left seeing that she was rolling over. Just as they were leaving the water began to run in the cabin window. At this critical moment the bin gave way and overboard went somewhere from two to three thousand bushels of oats. When she had light[en]ed herself she soon righted and stood once more on her bottom."

This entry of a near sinking, although dramatic, was not typical of the routine of the canal boat family. The journals more often describe the regular comings and goings on lake, canal, and rivers as the Bartleys, Chubbs and their fellow travelers seek the best loads and destinations to allow them to generate a profit for their labor. The journals have been painstakingly transcribed by Barbara Bartley, Theodore's great grand-daughter-in-law and are now being carefully read and edited by Russell Bellico and the author, who are working to publish an abridged edition.

RYAN BOATYARD WHITEHALL N.Y.

(above left)
John "Jack" Ryan's Boatyard,
Whitehall, New York, circa 1890.
Courtesy Canal Society of New York State.

(above right)
Theodore Bartley, circa 1895.
Theodore was also a skilled gunsmith.
Courtesy Barbara Bartley.

(right)
In Tow Down the Narrows of Lake Champlain.
Photograph by Howard Pyle,
Courtesy Fort Ticonderoga Museum.

Burlington Schooner Project Opening Day, June 21, 2001.
From the LCMM Collection.

⊰ *The Burlington Schooner Project* ⊱

In the fall of 2000, the Lake Champlain Maritime Museum launched its plan to construct the first canal schooner built on Lake Champlain in over 100 years. This endeavor, the most ambitious ever undertaken by the LCMM, was christened the Burlington Schooner Project. With a leadership gift from Mac and Lois McClure, and the encouragement of Burlington Mayor Peter Clavelle and Vermont Senator Patrick Leahy, the LCMM Board of Trustees voted to implement the project. The Lake Champlain Transportation Company (LCTC) graciously offered the museum the ideal shipbuilding site at their historic King Street Ferry Dock on the Burlington waterfront. With this positive momentum, our staff undertook this challenging project.

To meet the challenges of building the schooner and opening the project up to the public, LCMM brought together a talented group of problem solvers, boat builders, interpreters, and volunteers. Longtime LCMM facilities manager Don Dewees was recruited to be the first year's project manager and Captain Mike LaVecchia was selected as the assistant project manager. Rob Thompson, a talented Vermont boat builder, was hired to provide technical support. Elisa Nelson and Matt Davis were brought on as educators. It was an all hands effort to launch the project. Much of our initial work focused on converting a former lumber warehouse into a shipyard and designing a comprehensive historical exhibit for the site.

⊰ *The First Season* ⊱

The replica is modeled after the two 1862-class canal schooners sunk in Burlington Bay. She is 88 feet long with a beam of 14½ feet and a hold-depth of six feet. The scale of the project led us to immediately start a major effort to locate the thousands of board feet of lumber that would be required to build the schooner. The wood of choice, both historically and presently, is white oak, a strong, dense, rot-resistant wood that was once plentiful in the Champlain Valley. This slow-growing shipbuilding wood has been heavily lumbered and few stands of the valuable trees remain. We calculated that we needed more than 30,000 board feet of white oak to frame and plank the hull completely. The decks would be white pine. David Brynn, the Addison County Forester and the director of Vermont Family Forests, assisted in our search; however, it soon became apparent that we could not complete our cut-list in the Champlain Valley. We extended our

Burlington Shipyard Sign Being Installed Atop of Former Woodbury Lumber Shed, 2001.
From the LCMM Collection.

137

search and found a logging outlet in New York State's Catskill Mountains that could supply much of what we needed. In the end, and in light of the difficulty in procuring large quantities of good oak, we chose to incorporate more pine into the schooner's planking.

As appropriate trees were located, they were purchased and trucked to Adam and Ruth Weselow's sawmill in Morrisville, Vermont. Here the logs were custom cut into the dimensions needed to build the schooner. Back at the shipyard, Rob Thompson was building the schooner's yawl boat, a small tender that any large vessel requires for a multitude of chores. After much discussion, we chose to build a Connecticut River drag boat, as described by America's preeminent naval architect Howard Chapelle. It was the perfect design for our needs. We also began searching for the white spruce trees of the right dimension to be shaped into the schooner's spars. These trees were located in Danville, Vermont, at the Joel Currier Family Tree Farm and brought to the Shipyard for hewing into the schooner's mast, booms and gaffs.

We officially opened our Burlington Schooner Shipyard on June 21, 2001, and the site quickly proved the perfect setting for our enthusiastic crew of staff and volunteers. It was also apparent that we had touched a responsive chord with the

Don Dewees and Joel Currier Examine Trees for Spars, 2001.
From the LCMM Collection.

Spar Timbers Arrive in Burlington, 2001.
From the LCMM Collection.

(above)
Boat Builder Steve Paige Explains the Project to a Group of Students, 2002.
From the LCMM Collection.

(right)
Mike LaVecchia Looks on as Rob Thompson Shapes a Spar Using an Adze, 2001.
From the LCMM Collection.

(far right)
Rob Thompson Examines a Large White Oak Crook, 2001.
From the LCMM Collection.

Volunteer Al Stiles Works on the Spars, 2001.
Photograph by Eric Bessette, LCMM Collection.

public: during those first months we hosted more than 12,000 visitors. By the end of the first season we had located most of our timber needs and were amassing large stacks of lumber at the site so that it could begin to dry for use in the spring. The spruce trees from Danville were transformed into beautifully proportioned spars, giving the first sense of scale to the schooner.

The highlight of the first season's work was the completion and launching of the yawl boat. This 17-foot boat is a beautifully proportioned and functional tender. Rob Thompson's skill, coupled with the dedication of volunteers, produced a boat that was not only functional, but also an aesthetically pleasing work of art. In honor of the McClure's support of the project, and as a reflection of Lois's lifelong love of the lake, the new canal schooner would be named *Lois McClure.* It did not take long for Don Dewees's suggested name for the yawl boat, *Mac,* to be adopted. With his family surrounding him for his 82nd birthday, Mac McClure had the pleasure of seeing the new boat christened, launched, and sailed for the first time. All who have sailed or rowed *Mac* declare her to be a great piece of work.

The Canal Boat's Tender During Construction.
From the LCMM Collection.

Interpreter Elisa Nelson Explains to a Visitor How the Tree is Transformed into a Mast, 2001.
From the LCMM Collection.

A Young Steersman on the O.J. Walker *Steering Station Exhibit, 2001.* This "shin-cracker" steering assembly made by Paul Nelson will be installed on the new schooner.
From the LCMM Collection.

A Group Gathers to Hear How the Schooner's Timber was Gathered From Regional Forests, 2001.
From the LCMM Collection.

Don Dewees Rows as Mac McClure Enjoys the Inaugural Ride on the Just Launched Schooner Tender Mac, *2001.*
From the LCMM Collection.

The First Year of the Project was Spent in Designing and Producing the Historical Exhibits that Placed the Project in Perspective, 2001.
From the LCMM Collection.

The Schooner Lois McClure *in the Morning Sun, June 2003.*
Photograph by Nick LaVecchia, from the LCMM Collection.

142

⊰ *The Second Season* ⊱

Building on the preparations during the first season, the second year focused on building the schooner. Our boat building team was enlarged with the recruitment of Paul Rollins, a professional Maine shipwright, as our lead builder. Steve Page, a professional shipwright from Williston, Vermont, was recruited, and together with Rob Thompson, these three provided the expertise to begin transforming our piles of lumber into the first canal schooner built in over 100 years. The boat builders were ably supported by returning staff members Mike LaVecchia, Matt Davis, and Elisa Nelson as well as new crew members John Connell, Erika Place, and Lianna Tennal. This talented staff, with the assistance of an army of volunteers, was poised to provide the skill and energy to build the schooner.

Before we could actually build the schooner we needed plans to build from. The schooner's design was based on *General Butler* and *O.J. Walker,* two archaeological examples documented over many years of underwater examination. This accumulated archaeological information was translated into formal plans by naval architect Ron Smith, and Ray Sargeant, our own resident expert. Our experienced boat builders worked through the drafted designs and lofted the final detailed construction drawings that became the templates for shaping the various timbers for the hull.

As we began to layout and build the schooner, refinement and discussions of construction details not captured in our archaeological studies led to a revelation. The three shipwrights, none of whom were certified divers, would be greatly aided if they could see *General Butler* and *O.J. Walker* for themselves. We offered the boat building team an opportunity to become certified SCUBA divers and they all jumped at the chance. Their course of instruction culminated with successful dives to *O.J. Walker* and *General Butler.* Their ability to actually see the original 1862-class canal schooners resting on the bottom of Burlington Harbor provided them a unique insight into the project and an appreciation, in particular, for the unusual curved shape of the stern.

⊰⊱

Students Learn to Cut Wood with an Old Cross-cut Saw, 2002.
From the LCMM Collection.

Staff Member John Connell Fits a Floor Timber into the Chine Log, 2002.
From the LCMM Collection.

143

Work began to shape the massive piles of lumber into the structural timbers for schooner's bottom. Two large chine log timbers, 10 inches square and 60 feet long, were scarfed together. The chine logs along with the keel and keelson, both 15 inches by 6 inches would be the boat's backbone. Floor timbers, 5 inches square, were notched into the chine logs using classic timber framing techniques. Shorter floor timbers were fashioned to go around the 18-foot long centerboard trunk.

We chose to build the schooner's bottom upside-down to make the job of fastening the oak bottom planking easier. By the end of June, construction had progressed beautifully, and it was time to flip the schooner's bottom over. We chose Brown's Crane and Rigging from Bristol, Vermont, to perform the delicate operation. With three cranes providing the muscle, the complicated process took just over three hours. With the bottom now in its proper orientation, the progress from this point on was

Boat Builder Rob Thompson, 2002. Rob works on the keel scarf with a chisel. From the LCMM Collection.

Boat Builder Paul Rollins, 2003. Paul examines timber being made ready for the schooner. Photograph by Nick LaVecchia, from the LCMM Collection.

Boat Building Apprentice Lianna Tennal, 2002. Lianna helps prepare the keel scarf for joining. From the LCMM Collection.

Boat Builder Steve Page, 2002. Steve positions a chine timber. From the LCMM Collection.

explosive. Many of the futtocks needed to support the sides had already been produced and, as these vertical elements were added, the body of the new schooner began to take shape. The most impressive addition to the shape came when the stem, a massive piece of white oak, was raised. With the stem in place and the framing nearing completion, staff and visitors alike could now visualize the schooner's size and shape. As the season progressed, the historic schooners we had studied for so long underwater began to materialize in our shipyard.

❦

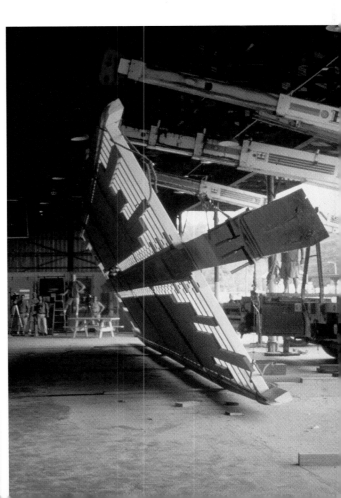

(Above)
The Bottom of the Schooner Before Being Turned Over, 2002.
From the LCMM Collection.

(Right)
The Turning of the Bottom of the Hull was a Major Moment in the Project, 2002.
From the LCMM Collection.

(Left)
The Stem was Raised Shortly After the Bottom was Flipped, 2002.
From the LCMM Collection.

(Below)
A Steam Box to Prepare the Heavy Oak Planks for Bending into Position was Provided by Harry Atkinson and Friends, 2003.
Photograph By Nick LaVecchia, from the LCMM Collection.

The Frames Began to Rise as Soon as the Bottom was Turned, 2002.
From the LCMM Collection.

*Boat Builders Prepare the Transom
for the Rudder Posts, 2002.*
From the LCMM Collection.

By the season's end, the schooner's skeleton was completed and the crew began fastening the outer planking. School groups and youth programs were incorporated into the project, while the museum's longboats, kayaks, canoes, and *Mac* were providing a whole series of programs for the community on the Burlington waterfront. As we closed the shipyard down for the winter, plans for completing construction next season were already under discussion, as was the summer 2004 launch and the schooner's Inaugural Lake Tour and Grand Journey. The future of the Burlington Schooner Project came into better focus everyday.

*The Frames Went Up and the Centerboard
was Put into Position, 2002.*
From the LCMM Collection.

(right)
By the Close of the 2002 Season, Great Progress had Been Made on the Schooner's Frame, 2002.
From the LCMM Collection.

(far right)
Hull Planking Begun, 2002.
Here Mac McClure works with David Minert to secure a plank.
From the LCMM Collection.

(below)
By the Beginning of the 2003 Season, the Frame of the Schooner was Largely Completed, 2003.
Photograph by Nick LaVecchia, from the LCMM Collection.

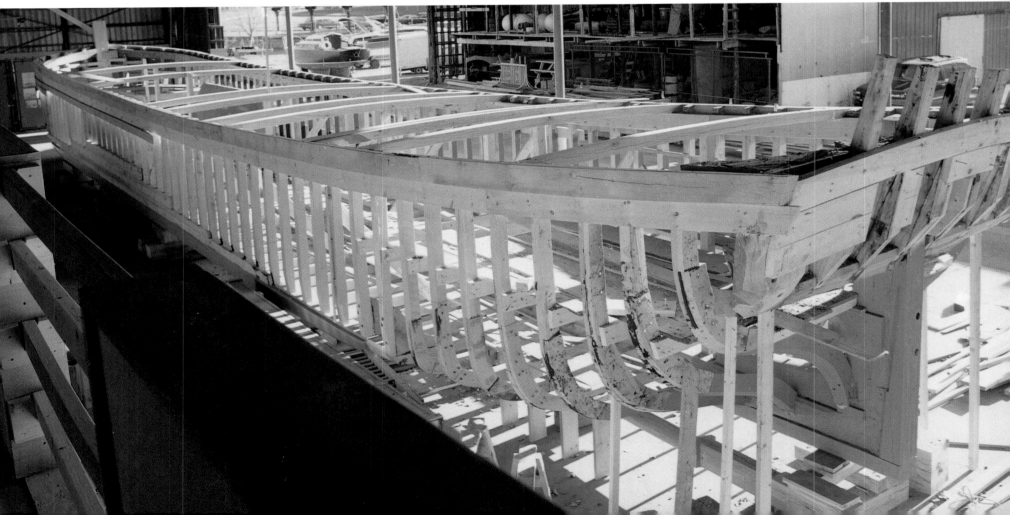

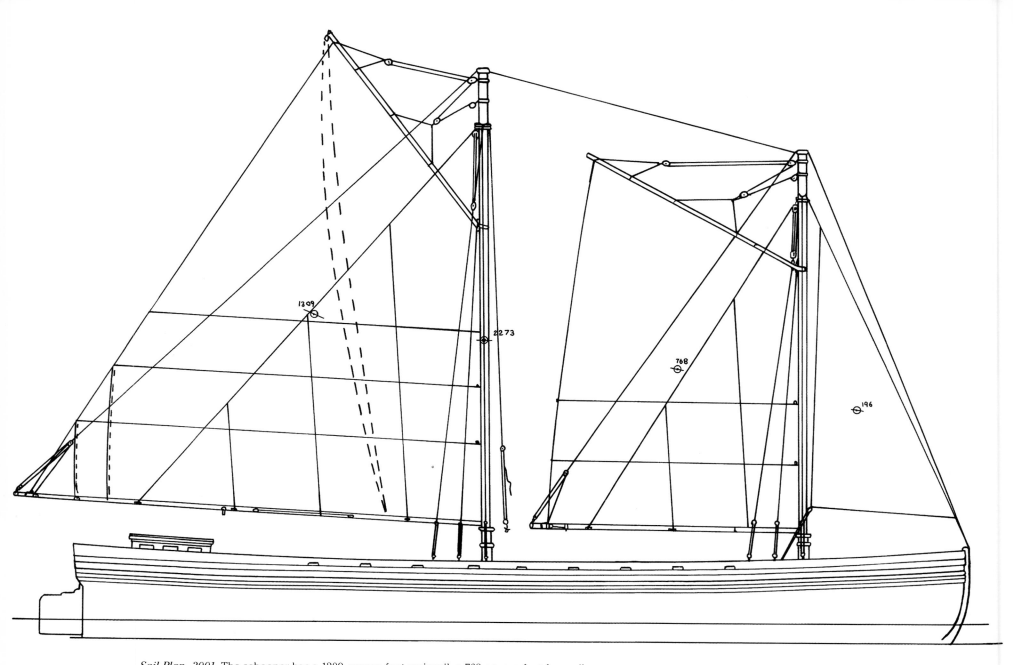

Sail Plan, 2001. The schooner has a 1309-square-foot mainsail, a 768-square-foot fore sail, and a 196-square-foot jib. Reef points in the main and fore sails, allow them to be reduced in size in stormy conditions. The main sail will have three reef points and the fore sail will have two reef points. This sail plan suggests that historically the ship captain and one or two crew could handle one of these schooners.

Drawn by Ron Smith, from the LCMM Collection.

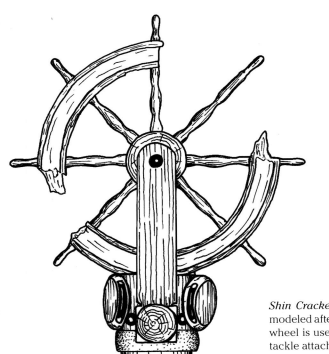

⊰ *Plans for the Schooner* Lois McClure ⊱

For hundreds of years shipwrights have used two-dimensional plans to depict the complex three-dimensional vessels they want to build. Examining the archaeological studies of the canal schooners *General Butler* and *O.J. Walker* formed the basis of generating plans for the new schooner. Also utilized were historical information and photographs. Naval architect Ron Smith took this information and developed the first set of preliminary plans. During the lofting and construction process, boat builder Rob Thompson, with input from our other talented boat builders, used the accumulated information to create a new set of plans. One unique feature of our project is the existence of two sunken canal boats to use as full-size models within a half-mile of our building site. Regular visits by the LCMM archaeologists to *General Butler* and *O.J. Walker* have helped provide construction details not captured in the original study.

Shin Cracker Wheel. The schooner's shin cracker is modeled after the one documented on *O.J. Walker*. The wheel is used to rotate the rudderpost via block and tackle attached to the short tiller and the bulwarks. Drawn by Kevin Crisman and Adam Loven.

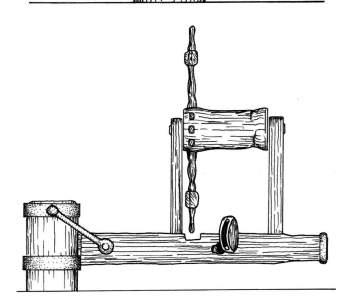

Centerboard. One of the canal schooner's most unique features is the centerboard. Being a flat-bottomed design, the centerboard provides lateral resistance for the schooner when under sail. The centerboard pivots at the forward end, allowing it to be lowered when sailing and raised while traveling in the canal. Drawn by Adam Loven.

Canal Schooner Lois McClure

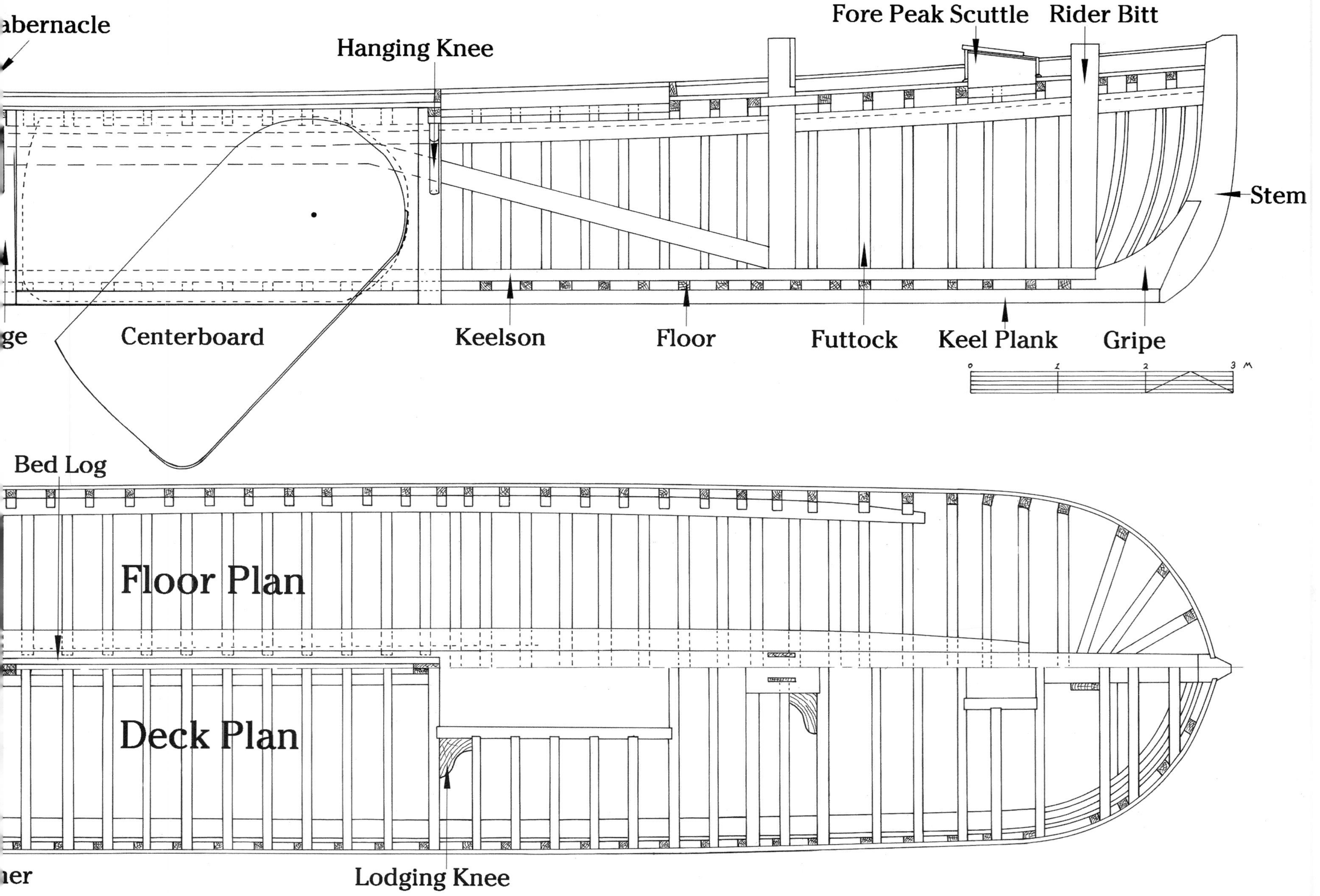

Tabernacle

Fore Peak Scuttle

Rider Bitt

Hanging Knee

Stem

ge

Centerboard

Keelson

Floor

Futtock

Keel Plank

Gripe

0   1   2   3 M

Bed Log

Floor Plan

Deck Plan

her

Lodging Knee

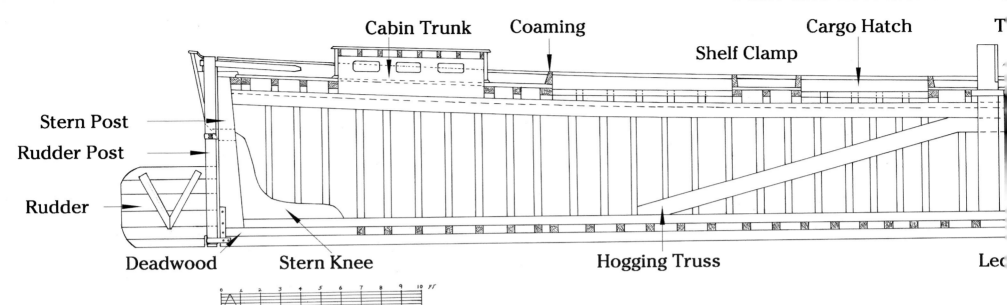

Cabin Trunk Coaming Cargo Hatch T

Shelf Clamp

Stern Post

Rudder Post

Rudder

Deadwood Stern Knee Hogging Truss Le

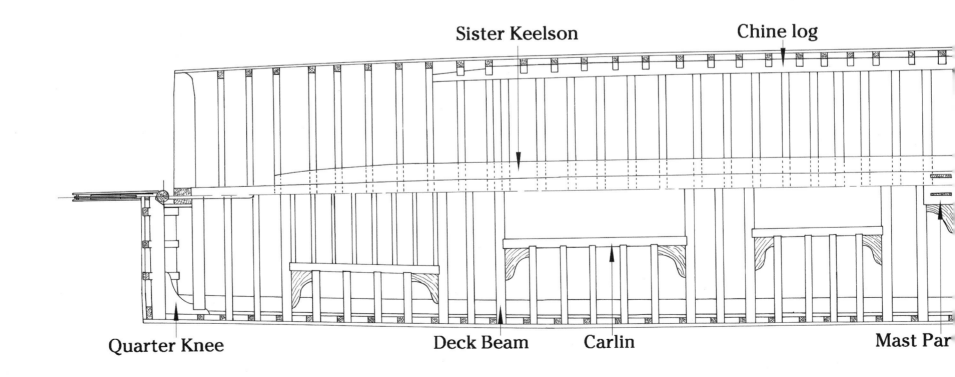

Sister Keelson Chine log

Quarter Knee Deck Beam Carlin Mast Par

The Launching of Lois McClure.
Drawn by Ernie Haas, from the LCMM Collection.

⊰ *The Launching of* Lois McClure ⊱

Once construction of the schooner is completed, *Lois McClure* will make the transition from a wooden object created in the shipyard to a living watercraft. In the summer of 2004, we will work with that rare breed of engineer—the house mover—to lift the schooner and construct a trailer under her so that she can be carefully guided out the north end of the shipyard construction shed. The schooner will then be paraded to the water's edge where she will be readied for launching. The launching of any vessel is an exciting moment and we plan to make the launching of *Lois McClure* a grand community celebration. We expect thousands of people to attend the launching and all manner of music and special events. An actual launching is always a tense affair, with history recording a high percentage of mishaps. We hope to avoid that particular connection with history.

Once the schooner is christened, blessed and encouraged into her new element, she will be docked for a three-day public celebration, giving people an opportunity to come aboard. Our crew will then take over the ship and complete the final stages of fitting out and getting *Lois McClure* ready for sail.

Captain Roger Taylor, 2003.
Photograph by Don Dewees.

We are privileged to have the thoughts of Roger Taylor, former captain of LCMM's Revolutionary War replica *Philadelphia II*, on his past replica experiences and his future command of *Lois McClure*. Roger comes to us as a twenty-year veteran of the U.S. Navy, former Editorial Director of the U.S. Naval Institute, Annapolis, Maryland, and founder of the International Marine Publishing Co. in Camden, Maine. He is the author of seven books and many articles on boat design and seamanship and is currently writing a biography of the yacht designer, L. Francis Herreshoff, to be published by the Mystic Seaport Museum.

Two Crew Members Get Ready to Set
Philadelphia II's *Topmast, 1991.*
From the LCMM Collection.

⊰ *A View from the Quarterdeck* ⊱
by Roger Taylor

As I sit down to write about the Lake Champlain Maritime Museum's two wonderful replica vessels, I was going to say that the most challenging aspect of commanding the *Philadelphia II* replica was maneuvering a 55-foot by 17-foot vessel with a dead-flat bottom and no vertical surface underwater. But I soon realized that the biggest challenge, as always, was leadership.

Philadelphia II's raw crew had not been together on board for ten minutes before we had our first injury that drew blood. Our second occurred before the day was out. Neither was serious; each provided an object lesson. Clearly we would have to slow down and put safety before all else. We had no further accidents, serious or otherwise, in two full seasons of operation. We had a great group of core crewmen who stayed with the vessel throughout each summer's cruising (of course they seemed very young to me!) and a great group of volunteers who came and went on a regular basis. The challenge was to achieve the necessary teamwork for successful rowing or sailing on a given day with the combination of knowledge and inexperience of that day's crew.

We worked together to move the vessel safely on schedule where we wanted her to go, despite the vagaries of Lake Champlain weather, which brings us back to her flat bottom. You can point *Philadelphia II* whichever way you want to point her, but she's going to go to leeward, with the wind. She was great at making leeway. I was often thankful that my first command, a half century earlier, was in a seven-foot, flat-bottomed punt; otherwise I might have had some nasty surprises.

On our first day heading up the lake toward Whitehall, we were sailing toward the opening under the Crown Point Bridge,

153

when the wind changed enough so that *Philadelphia II* started crabbing toward the bridge abutment to leeward. We had to get out half a dozen of her long, heavy sweeps and put them into concerted action without delay to give the vessel enough headway to overcome the leeway she loved. The new crew responded well to the situation, and the Crown Point Bridge stood undamaged.

Later in the campaign, when the crew had gained experience, they saved the vessel from a potential dismasting. We had left the shelter of Valcour Island (where Benedict Arnold had so wisely sought shelter with the squadron that included the original *Philadelphia*) and were heading north on the lake. The wind was blowing hard from the south, and we had to steer well east of north to keep from blowing down onto Cumberland Point. The farther behind we had left the shelter of Valcour Island, the more *Philadelphia II* began to roll in the seas that had built up out on the lake. We were not worried about the guns; we always had them well secured when underway. But this much rolling was new to the vessel, and the mast and yards began to sway and gyrate dangerously. Orders rang out and the crew ran to swifter, braces, lifts all the lines that led aloft to the ends of the spars, and heaved them up taut as hard as they could. And then we quickly went round and tightened them up some more. Mast and yards, thus supported, rolled docilely with the vessel. The crew saved their vessel from damage in the most precarious situation she had faced. Making all that rigging bar-taut before leaving harbor would have been second nature to Horatio Hornblower or Jack Aubrey, but we were twentieth-century sailors running an eighteenth-century ship.

Lois McClure will present many of the same challenges offered by *Philadelphia II.* A vessel's real size should be measured by displacement, and *Lois McClure* will outweigh *Philadelphia II* by a factor of four. When trying to make the perfect eggshell landing at the dock, the one that does not break the shell of the egg placed between hull and pier, *Lois McClure*'s hull will have four times the force of *Philadelphia II*'s at the same speed. Undoubtedly, *Lois McClure* will not go exactly where you point her, but, with her big centerboard lowered, she will certainly go closer to where she is pointing than would *Philadelphia II.* Her fore-and-aft schooner rig will give her far more maneuverability under sail than her square-rigged predecessor, and her foresail will be her security blanket: when the wind whistles, you can take

(left)
Captain Roger Taylor Instructs the Crew Aboard Philadelphia II, *1991.*
From the LCMM Collection.

(below)
Philadelphia II *Navigates Under the Champlain Bridge, in 1991.*
From the LCMM Collection.

in the mainsail and jib and sail with just the foresail, a relatively small sail close enough to the middle of the vessel so it can be used all by itself. We will be able to tuck her into "foresail harbor," as the Gloucester fisherman used to say.

In the modern world of schedules, both replicas need a motorized towboat for days when it is necessary to cover miles with no wind or with wind from ahead, or, in the case of *Lois McClure*, for canal travel. Towing operations on *Lois McClure* will be similar to what they were on *Philadelphia II:* tow "on the hip" in calm and sheltered water and from ahead in rougher going, steering from the towboat, not from the towed vessel. Remember that factor of four when judging pace and distance.

But it will be the people who will make the operations of *Lois McClure* successful, just as was the case with *Philadelphia II.* Core crew and volunteers will have to work as a team, will have to put safety before all else, and will have to be willing to devote themselves to their vessel. The old Quaker ship captain had it about right, "Six days shalt thou labor and do all that are able; and on the seventh, mend thy tarpaulin and overhaul thy cable."

Philadelphia II *at Whitehall, New York, 1991.* Two young visitors stand at the tiller. Note the tugboat and oil barge in the background entering Lock 12.
From the LCMM Collection.

Philadelphia II *Underway on Lake Champlain, 1991.*
From the LCMM Collection.

⚓ *The Inaugural Lake Tour and the Grand Journey* ⚓

By Alan McKibben, coauthor of the *Hudson River Journey, An Artist's Perspective* and of the *Cruising Guide to the Hudson River, Lake Champlain, and the St. Lawrence River.*

The idea of recreating the journey made by historic sailing canal boats more than a century ago was born of the museum staff's first discussions about the possibility of building a working, full-sized replica of a sailing canal schooner. Making the nearly 300-mile journey from Burlington Bay to New York City along Lake Champlain, the Champlain Canal, and the Hudson River would bring the history of this corridor to life. This journey would be a once-in-a-lifetime experience for the crew of the *Lois McClure.*

A typical canal boat was operated by a single family with perhaps a paid crewman. For our journey we will have a larger crew, consisting of a captain, two mates, a cook, up to five museum volunteers acting as deckhands, and two members of the museum's staff. This expanded crew will enable us to meet the challenges of learning to sail and maneuver a boat that is both large and none too nimble and to support the journey's educational programs at her ports of call.

Onboard, *Lois McClure* will have the look and feel of an authentic canal boat. Her layout, both above and below decks, will be similar to her predecessors'. Representative cargo will be carried, to add to the authenticity of the journey as well as to add weight and the resulting stability. Some of her equipment will also be authentic, although there will be some twenty-first century additions such as a holding tank for the onboard toilet, Dacron sails instead of canvas, and radios for communications.

Canal boats usually traveled nonstop, stopping only to pick up or discharge cargo; our schedule, however, will allow *Lois McClure* to make frequent stops at ports along the route. Here visitors will come onboard to get a close look at how these boats worked, what cargos they carried, and how their crews lived.

Canal Boats in Burlington, circa 1890.
From a private collection.

The Canal Schooner General Butler *Under Sail.*
By Ernie Haas, private collection.

Lake Champlain, From St. Albans, circa 1880.
From a private collection.

Our Inaugural Tour will be on Lake Champlain, revisiting several historic ports that were once the familiar territory for sailing canal boats. We plan to go first to St. Albans Bay, Vermont, the harbor within the Inland Sea where the original *Gleaner* was built and launched in 1823. *Gleaner* of St. Albans was the very first boat to complete the passage from Lake Champlain through the new canal to the Hudson River in October 1823. From St. Albans we expect to travel to Rouses Point, New York, historically and currently the U.S. Customs point-of-entry for boats traveling south from Canada. We will visit Plattsburgh, New York, which Julius Rugar, the second owner of *General Butler* called home, and Essex, New York, where *General Butler* and so many other sailing canal boats were built at the shipyard of Hoskins and Ross. Next we will visit the historic harbor Westport, New York, home port of the ill-fated *Troy* of Westport, the canal schooner that foundered in 1825 with loss of all aboard. We will return to Burlington and then travel to LCMM's home

A Standard and Sailing Canal Boat in Plattsburgh Harbor, circa 1898.
From "Historic Lake Champlain"
by Seneca Ray Stoddard.

port at Basin Harbor. The new schooner *Lois McClure* and her crew will then embark for the southern end of Lake Champlain. She will pass through the river-like southern lake, past the Narrows of Dresden, home to the Chubbs, Bartleys and Bartholomews, mariners who operated sailing canal boats along this same route for decades. Then, it will be on to the Fiddler's Elbow, the home of Cora Archambault, who will be taken aboard for a visit at Whitehall, New York, the southern limit of navigation on Lake Champlain and the northern end of the Champlain Canal.

Whitehall first rose to maritime prominence as the construction site of the colonial fleet that opposed the British at the Battle of Valcour in 1776. With the completion of the Champlain Canal, Whitehall became one of the lake's major commercial ports. Before the creation of the canal, the route between Lake Champlain and the Hudson River required a time-consuming and bone-jarring passage, over both land and water, via Lake George. With the opening of the

Canal Boats at Whitehall, New York, circa 1890.
Courtesy Canal Society of New York State.

canal it was possible to move bulky cargoes quickly and economically. The present sixty-two mile long canal follows an excavated channel for its first twenty miles before joining the Hudson for the remaining forty-two miles to Troy. Canal traffic passes through twelve locks, which combine first to lift vessels 44 feet to the height of land and then to lower them 153 feet to reach tidewater at Troy.

After visiting Whitehall the schooner will return to Burlington until she embarks on her 2005 Grand Journey. As the 2005 navigation season opens *Lois McClure* will once again display her colors around Lake Champlain before entering the canal at Whitehall. This will be the official start of her Grand Journey through the canal and Hudson River to New York City.

After departing Whitehall, canal traffic passes the historic villages of Fort Ann, Comstock, Fort Edward, Fort Miller, Schuylerville, Mechanicville, and Waterford. The canal brought an economic windfall to the villages it passed through. Being able to import and export goods easily gave merchants on the canal an advantage over their inland competitors. As a result, thriving waterfronts developed along the canal. *Lois McClure* will stop at two of these villages, Fort Edward and Mechanicville. Farther south, at Waterford, the Mohawk River and the Erie Canal enter the Hudson. Extending 332 miles to the west, the Erie Canal connects the Hudson River and the Champlain Canal to the Great Lakes. Long a crossroads for river and canal traffic, Waterford will be a stop for *Lois McClure* before she passes through the last lock to navigate the Hudson River.

To Native Americans the river we call the Hudson was known as the "river that flows two ways." Giovanni da Verrazano was the first European to catch a glimpse of New York Harbor. Eighty-five years later, in 1609, Henry Hudson sailed his *Half Moon* far upriver, until he ran aground, in search of the elusive Northwest Passage to the riches of China and the Indies. Using the ship's boat, the master's mate continued to explore another day upriver until he found more shoals and depths of less than seven feet, probably in the vicinity of today's Albany. Hudson's discovery marked the start of colonization by the Dutch and English that continued until the American Revolution.

Canal Boat Traveling Through Comstock, New York on the Champlain Canal, circa 1880.
Courtesy Canal Society of New York State.

Canal Boats Tied up at Waterford, New York, circa 1890.
Courtesy Canal Society of New York State.

(above)
Lighthouse on the Hudson, circa 1840.
By W.H. Bartlett, from a private collection.

(below)
Albany, Capital of the State of New York, circa 1820.
Detail of Plate No. 13 by Jacques Milbert, from a private collection.

A View of Hudson and the Catskill Mountains, circa 1820.
Plate No. 12 by Jacques Milbert, from a private collection.

The Coal Depot at Rondout, New York, 1867.
Sketched by Theodore R. Davis from *Harper's Weekly*, December 14, 1867.

The first Dutch outpost, Fort Nassau, was positioned just south of Albany to exploit the fur trade in the Catskill and Adirondack Mountains and in the Mohawk River Valley. New Amsterdam, renamed New York when the English took over, was established at the mouth of the river to protect Dutch interests in the Hudson Valley and to serve as the port for the colony's transatlantic trade.

The Hudson had great appeal for early explorers, traders, and settlers. With the exception of just a few kinks as it passes through the Highlands, it is nearly straight, flowing in a north-south direction into the heart of what was, 400 years ago, a vast wilderness. It has an immense, protected harbor at its mouth capable of sheltering the largest fleet of ships. It is deep enough to allow deep-draft, ocean-going vessels to travel far upriver. And, of course, the tidal currents provide a welcome boost for the patient mariner willing to wait for the push of the tides.

For the first 200 years, Hudson River travel was dominated by the Hudson River sloop, typically seventy feet long with a large main sail set on a single mast. At first they had leeboards in the Dutch style, then later centerboards such as that used by *Lois McClure*. With the maiden voyage of Robert Fulton's *North River Steam Boat* in 1807, steam became king on the river, with all manner of steam-powered vessels transporting passengers and cargo. *North River Steam Boat* made her initial trip from New York City to Albany in thirty-two hours. Competition between rival steamship lines continually reduced the time for this passage until the Day Line promised an all daylight trip from New York City to Albany. The opening of the Champlain (1823) and Erie (1825) Canals began an era of dazzling river commerce as goods and passengers passed between New York City, Quebec City, Montreal, Buffalo, the North American West, and Europe.

The canal era also introduced a new vessel to the Hudson: the canal boat. Ungainly when compared to the sloops and steamboats, they were a commercial success, transporting large quantities of goods on the connecting canals, rivers, and lakes. Large tows of canal boats and barges were collected at Albany or across the river at Rensselaer and were pulled down the Hudson by towboats, which were often converted side-wheeler passenger steamboats. Sailing canal boats, such as *Lois McClure* either joined one of these tows or proceeded alone under their own sail-power.

Both the Champlain and Erie Canals have been rerouted and modernized since they were first built. Changes were made to accommodate larger boats with their larger carrying capacities and to make the locks more efficient by reducing their numbers, increasing their lift, and speeding up their operation. When they were first dug, both canals operated from the Albany Basin. Imagine the lively scene of barges, tugs, steamers, ferries, canal boats, mules, horses, and oxen, crews, and families all focused on boats exiting and entering the canals, with the widest variety of cargo! Present-day Albany has a popular waterfront park and a boatyard where *Lois McClure*'s masts, which have been lowered for passage through the canal, will be raised and her sails hoisted. Once beyond the Albany Basin, heading down river, *Lois McClure* will quickly pass beyond the deep-water port of Albany and the sites of the early Dutch Fort Nassau and its successor, Fort Orange.

Nearly four hundred years of history and commerce have taken place along these waters. However, even today, once south of Albany, the river seems surprisingly undeveloped with marshes and wetlands extending along both shores. Only the occasional village or factory interrupts this pastoral setting. The once thriving river landings, with the names of Castleton, Schodack, Coeymans, New Baltimore, Kinderhook, and Coxsackie boast homes that were built by prosperous Dutch settlers. This is a region where travelers in the nineteenth century wrote of still hearing Dutch spoken. The villages of Hudson and Athens face each other across a wide expanse where a mid-river lighthouse warns of shoals. This is the first of four distinctive lighthouses of house-like structures—with light-towers attached—which are encountered on the trip down river.

For the next twenty miles the western shore is dominated by the Catskill Mountains, home to Washington Irving's Rip Van Winkle and the Hudson River School of landscape painting, source of drinking water for New York City, and long a destination for vacation travelers. The Village of Catskill, on Catskill Creek, once boasted an active waterfront, which, in addition to passengers, handled cargoes of shale, iron, leather, farm produce, and of course, one of the most often carried cargos, ice for the iceboxes of New York City. With Catskill's Landing close to the edge of the channel, it is possible that any passing vessel heading down river with room for more cargo stopped to see if there was any freight to be carried.

Farther south, as the river widens, the shores are more developed; farms and villages are replaced by mansions and cities: Saugerties, Kingston, Hyde Park, Poughkeepsie, and Newburgh. These too, began as single homesteads or settlements, depending on the river for transportation and contact with the outside world. Kingston was the state capital during the Revolution after the British captured New York City, and it later was burned to the ground by the British in a failed attempt to seize control of the entire Hudson Valley. Kingston became an important port on the Hudson when the 108-mile long, 107-lock Delaware and Hudson Canal was completed in 1828. This route, which connected Kingston's Rondout Creek with the Delaware River at Honesdale, Pennsylvania, provided a water route for coal, which not only was delivered to New York City, but also was exported to Canada through the Champlain or Northern waterways. The Hudson River Maritime Museum, with a fleet of historic vessels, is located on the Strand at Kingston. *Lois McClure* will dock here and her crew will participate in museum activities.

The City of Newburgh boasts a recently revitalized waterfront, where *Lois McClure* will stop at a pier that was once a host to numerous river vessels. Newburgh Bay is the widest part of the river encountered to this point in the journey, but ahead the river seems to run headlong into the mountains. Storm King Mountain to the west and Break Neck Mountain to the east stand as sentinels at the Hudson River Highlands, where the Hudson cuts through the Appalachian Mountain chain. In the next few miles the river makes abrupt turns as it reaches its greatest depths (over 200 feet) and passes through "World's End" where early boatmen spied whirlpools and were often stymied by contrary winds. In the early days of the Revolution, General George Washington chose to fortify the Highlands against a British invasion. His forces stretched a chain across the river and erected forts, which were to become the United States Military Academy at West Point, the oldest continuously occupied U.S. military post and one of New York State's most popular tourist attractions. West Point's south dock will be one of *Lois McClure*'s most historic and spectacular stops.

The southern gateway to the Highlands is marked by Dunderberg Mountain and the city of Peekskill, which face each other across the

View From West Point, Hudson River, circa 1840.
By W.H. Bartlett, from a private collection.

river. Peekskill is home to the National Maritime Historical Society, which will host *Lois McClure* for another of her port visits. Below the Highlands, the river widens first in Haverstraw Bay and then in the Tappan Zee. These broad bays have a long history of development and use. Their shallow depths function as a nursery for aquatic life with many ocean fish beginning their lives here. Their clam-flats fed Native Americans for centuries. New York City is only twenty-five miles ahead and this region is a popular residential area for commuters who make their way each day to jobs in the city. This is also a region that became heavy with factories as manufacturers sought to be near their markets. Bricks, shoes, and cars have been built and shipped from the cities of Haverstraw, Ossining, Tarrytown, and Nyack.

So far the Hudson has been solely New York State's river. However, for the final twenty miles to its mouth, the boundary between New York and New Jersey runs right down the middle of the river; the west shore is New Jersey and the east shore is New York. The west shore from the Tappan Zee south is dominated by the rock cliffs of the Palisades, which rise up to 200 feet above the river and are for the most part undeveloped park land. Piermont is the last village before the Palisades; in the mid-1800s railroad developers built a mile-long pier across shallows here so that Pennsylvania coal could be off loaded from rail cars to barges for the trip to the furnaces of New York City. A string of villages line the east shore opposite the Palisades; once factory towns, they now host many posh suburbs: Irvington, Ardsley, Dobbs Ferry, Hastings, and Yonkers. Yonkers, once the center of one of

the earliest Dutch patroonships, is the home of the Hudson River Museum and boasts a spectacular replica of a Hudson River recreation pier. *Lois McClure* will make her last stop here before entering New York Harbor.

Canal boats coming down river were near the end of their journey at this point. Just south of Yonkers, Manhattan Island—the most central of New York City's five boroughs—is separated from the mainland by the Harlem River, which enters from the east at Spuyten Duyvil. In the years of peak waterfront activity, docks lined both shores of the Hudson from this point south, with those on the New Jersey shore connecting to competing railroad lines. Docks and basins were also found along both shores of the East River, which combines with the Hudson and Harlem Rivers to surround Manhattan Island. In the days of sail, square-riggers, schooners, and sloops docked on Manhattan's East River shore along Dock,

Peekskill Landing, Hudson River, circa 1839.
By W.H. Bartlett, from a private collection.

The Palisades-Hudson River, circa 1837.
By W.H. Bartlett, from a private collection.

Water, and South Streets. As the tows of canal boats neared the southern tip of Manhattan Island, they were dispersed by small harbor tugs to these docks, wharves, and basins to discharge and load cargoes.

At the end of her journey down the Hudson, *Lois McClure* will dock at the South Street Seaport Museum, site of the city's earliest docks on the East River. She will have retraced a journey made countless times in the past by vessels carrying cargo and passengers from Lake Champlain's Burlington Bay, through the Champlain Canal, and down the Hudson River to the thriving Port of New York.

Once she has returned from her Grand Journey to New York City, *Lois McClure* will begin her service to the community as Burlington's "Tall Ship." She will be docked on the waterfront where the new schooner will return the once common and distinctive canal schooner profile to the skyline. She will serve as a tangible and constant reminder of the wooden fleets that once dominated the landscape and the sailors and families that made their living traveling these inland waterways. She will be operated as an educational vessel with the public invited to board her, and school children to take part in a wide variety of onboard programs.

South Street and Harbor, Governor's Island in the Distance, circa 1895.
By an unidentified photographer, negative 50921. Note the New York & Lake
Champlain Transportation Co. sign on building center-right.
Collection of the New-York Historical Society.

The future of her operations under sail is yet to be written. Perhaps she will venture out the Erie Canal to Buffalo, New York, as some of our northern boats did when seeking good freight contracts. Perhaps she will continue to travel the lake as an ambassador for the nineteenth century commercial era and its mariners. What is clear is that once she is launched, as the first canal schooner built in more than a century, she will stimulate an awareness of a time and a way of life which are gone but should not be forgotten.

Canal Boats in New York Harbor with a Five-masted Schooner Going by, circa 1880.
Courtesy Canal Society of New York State.

South Street and Harbor, 2002.
Photograph by Mike LaVecchia, LCMM Collection.

167

Epilogue

As we approach the 400th Anniversary of Samuel de Champlain and Henry Hudson's journeys, it is fitting to reflect on events, past and present. Although many aspects of the region's rich history are preserved along the shorelines of Lake Champlain and the Hudson River, it is the recent discovery of a serene underwater archive of shipwrecks that holds almost limitless potential to expand our understanding of history. The collection is fragile, finite and in need of inventory, documentation and management for its long-term preservation. These submerged sites, all public resources, and their stories, need to be made accessible. The Lake Champlain Maritime Museum was established, in part, to serve as a place where the public could explore these stories.

The discovery of the shipwreck *General Butler* in 1980 made possible the rediscovery of Lake Champlain's sailing canal boats, a technological advance that coincided with the opening of the Champlain Canal in 1823. This once forgotten piece of our history is now better understood, revealing a dynamic economic era filled with canal boats, cargos and canal families. *General Butler* and the growing number sailing and standard canal boats being discovered on the lake and river bottom are serving as a stimulus for new research, writing, exhibits, and replica building. This is especially evident in the building of the canal schooner *Lois McClure*. The first of its type to be built in over 100 years, the schooner provides a tangible link to the nineteenth century world of canals, canal boats and canal people. This once almost invisible chapter in history is slowly being uncovered.

Our historical focus on Burlington Bay provides a dynamic example of the ebbs, flows and transitions of technology and its impact on the working waterfront. During the nineteenth century, Burlington Bay evolved into the most active commercial port on Lake Champlain, only to slide into a depression during the 1930s. Emerging from the depth of neglect, the waterfront today finds itself in a new period of cultural renaissance. As we approach the 400th anniversary of European arrival, the waterfront has been rediscovered, this time not for commerce, but for culture and recreation.

Windmill Point Lighthouse Relighting Day, August 7, 2002.
This lighthouse and the lighthouse on Isle La Motte are owned by the family of Lucky Clark. Both were relit in 2002.
Photograph by Pierre LaRocque, from the LCMM Collection.

In Burlington, the continued operation of lake ferry boats, the growing excursion boat fleet, the public and private investment represented in new waterfront housing, restaurants, the opening of the new ECHO-Leahy Center for Lake Champlain, the expanding presence of Main Street Landing, and building of the canal schooner *Lois McClure* all suggest a vibrant future. The Pine Street Barge Canal now offers the promise of an interpreted public natural-cultural area. As debate turns to the future of the "North Forty," the filled land formerly occupied by lumberyards and oil tanks, this waterfront space will help define the Burlington of the future. The long-studied Moran electric plant will move to center stage with powerful potential to bring yet more vibrant activity to the waterfront. Underwater Historic Preserves are poised to expand access to a number of newly discovered sites, and as if on cue, the historic lighthouses around the region have begun to be relit.

Writing this book made many new connections for me, and reminded me of some old ones. It reaffirmed the intimate connections between the region's waterways. My first home was in Nyack-on-the-Hudson and my last three decades have been spent exploring and working on and under Lake Champlain. I've had the privilege of working on the Lake Survey that has found so many of the ships that once traveled these waterways for commerce and conflict. I look forward to learning about the underwater collection now being discovered by research on the Hudson. Great challenges and opportunities still lie ahead for the proper management of our region's waterways. Threats from pollution, exotic species and past environmental behavior must still be actively addressed. But the growing recognition of the special nature of the region's waterways suggests that although the pendulum of public interest may swing back toward the center, it can never return to the environmental neglect of the past.

Art Cohn
Lake Champlain Maritime Museum
Ferrisburgh, Vermont
June 2003

A Statue Depicting Samuel de Champlain's Arrival in 1609.
This granite statue at St. Anne's Shrine in
Isle La Motte reflects the profound impact of
Europeans' arrival almost 400 years ago.
Photo by the author, from the LCMM Collection.

171

Glossary

Barge A large, unpowered, generally flat-bottomed boat towed by other craft and used as a freight-hauler or work platform.

Bateau (plural **bateaux**) A lightly built, flat-bottomed, double-ended boat.

Beam A dimension measured from side to side of a vessel.

Bilge The lowest point of a vessel's interior hull.

Boat An open vessel, usually small and without decks, intended for use in sheltered water.

Bow The forward end of a vessel.

Breakwater A structure, usually made of stone, wood or concrete, built to create a harbor or improve an existing one.

Cabin The living quarters of a vessel.

Cabin trunk The vertical side of a vessel's cabin located between the deck and the cabin roof.

Canal A man-made waterway or artificially improved river used for navigation.

Canal boat A boxy vessel designed to travel in a canal system. This type of vessel has no means of propulsion and must be towed or pushed by another vessel.

Carlin Pieces of squared timber fitted fore and aft between the deck beams of a wooden vessel.

Ceiling The internal planking of a vessel.

Centerboard A board or metal plate that moves vertically or pivots up and down in a slot in the keel; limits a vessel's lateral motion by increasing the surface area of the keel or keel plank.

Centerboard trunk A box-like structure used to house the centerboard which contains the pivot point of the centerboard.

Chine log A longitudinal timber at the angular junction of the side and bottom of a flat-bottomed vessel.

Clamp A thick ceiling strake used to provide longitudinal support.

Coaming The raised lip with which openings in the deck such as hatchways are framed to prevent water on deck from running into the hold.

Cultural resource A nonrenewable historical resource such as archaeological sites, artifacts, and standing structures.

Deadeye A round or pear-shaped block pierced by several holes, used mainly to secure the standing rigging of a vessel.

Deadwood The solid timbering in the bow and stern of a sailing vessel just above the keel where the lines narrow down to such an extent that the separate side timbers cannot each be accommodated.

Deck A platform extending horizontally from one side of a ship to the other.

Deck beam A timber mounted across a vessel from side to side to support the vessel's deck and provide lateral strength.

Draft The depth of a vessel's keel below the waterline when the vessel is loaded.

Floor timber A frame timber that crosses the keel and spans the bottom of a vessel.

Fore Located toward the front of a vessel.

Frame A transverse timber or group of timbers that creates the skeleton of a vessel and to which the hull planking and ceiling are fastened.

Futtock A frame timber that continues where the floor timber leaves off and continues up the side of a vessel.

Gondola A large, flat-bottomed, double-ended vessel propelled by oars or sails.

Gripe A curved piece joining the forward end of the keel to the lower end of the knee of the head.

Hanging knee A vertical L-shaped timber attached to the underside of a beam and the side of a vessel; used to connect and reinforce the junction of a deck beam with the side of the vessel.

Harbor A safe anchorage, protected from most storms; may be natural or man made; a place for docking and loading.

Hatch A deck opening in a vessel providing access to the space below.

Hogging truss A strong fore-and-aft structure built into a vessel to prevent the ends of a vessel from drooping.

Hold The lower interior part of a ship, where the cargo is stored.

Hull The structural body of a vessel, not including the superstructure, masts, or rigging.

Hull plank A thick board used to create the outer shell of a hull.

Inboard Toward the center of a vessel.

Keel The main longitudinal timber upon which the framework or skeleton of a hull is mounted; the backbone of a hull.

Keel plank A thick, central hull plank used in place of a keel.

Keelson An internal longitudinal timber, fastened on top of the frames above the keel for additional strength.

Knee An L-shaped timber used to strengthen the junction of two surfaces on different planes.

Leeboard One of a part of movable boards or plates attached to each side of a vessel to prevent slippage downwind.

Lodging knee A horizontally oriented knee.

Mast A large wooden pole that supports the sails of a vessel.

Mast partner Beams used to strengthen the opening in the deck where the mast passes through.

Mast tabernacle A timber assembly or housing that supports the mast at deck level. This feature was commonly used to support a hinged mast, like those used on sailing canal boats.

Mooring A permanent placement of an anchor, anchor chain, shackles, and buoy, necessary to anchor a vessel.

Plank A thick board used as sheathing on a vessel.

Port The left side of a vessel when facing forward.

Rider bitts Strong, upright timbers in the bow of a ship, to which lines were secured.

Rigging Hardware and equipment that support and control the spars and sails of a vessel.

Rudder A timber, or assembly of timbers, that could be rotated about an axis to control the direction of a vessel underway.

Rudder post A vertical timber to which the rudder is attached.

Sailing canal boat A boxy vessel with one or two fore-and-aft rigged masts that could be lowered when the vessel entered a canal system.

Schooner A fore-and-aft-rigged sailing vessel with two or more masts.

Scuttle A port cut into a ship to admit light and air.

Sheer The curvature of the deck from fore to aft, as seen from the side of the vessel.

Shelf clamp A thick ceiling strake used to provide longitudinal strength or support deck beams.

Sister keelson An auxiliary keelson fastened along side the main keelson (see also keelson).

Sloop A single-masted, fore-and-aft-rigged sail boat.

Sloop-rigged canal boat A boxy vessel with one fore-and-aft-rigged mast that could be lowered when the vessel entered a canal system.

Spike A large nail.

Stanchion An upright supporting post.

Starboard The right side of a vessel when facing forward.

Steamboat A vessel propelled by a steam engine.

Stem An upward curving timber or assembly of timbers attached to the forward end of the keel.

Stern The after end of a vessel.

Stern knee A standing knee used to join the keel to the sternpost.

Sternpost A vertical or upward curving timber or assembly of timbers stepped into, or scarfed to, the after end of the keel.

Tiller A handle attached to the rudderpost to steer a vessel.

Transom The transverse part of the stern of a vessel.

Underwater archaeology The archaeological study of submerged cultural resources.

Underwater cultural resource A nonrenewable historical resource that partially or entirely lies below water, such as submerged prehistoric archaeological sites, artifacts, bridges, piers, wharves, and shipwrecks.

Vessel A watercraft, larger than a rowboat, designed to navigate on open water.

Waterline The intersection of the vessel's hull and the water's surface.

Wharf A structure, parallel to the shore, for docking vessels.

Windlass A horizontal drum winch mounted on the bow of a vessel and supported by bitts or brackets; used for tasks such as hauling anchors, stepping masts, and moving cargo.

The La Chute River at Ticonderoga, New York, circa 1880. This photograph with a Canadian pin plat in the foreground and a Lake Champlain canal schooner center-right illustrates the volume of pulpwood moved around the region.

Courtesy Ticonderoga Historical Society.

Selected Bibliography

A Canalboat Primer on the Canals of New York State. Syracuse, NY: Canal Museum, 1981.

A Century of Progress: History of the Delaware and Hudson Company 1823–1923. Albany, NY: J.B. Lyon Company, 1925.

Adams, Arthur G. *The Hudson River Guidebook.* 2nd ed. New York: Fordham University Press, 1996.

Adams, Henry K. *A Centennial History of St. Albans, Vermont.* St. Albans, VT: Wallace Printing Company, 1889.

Allen, Charles E. *About Burlington Vermont.* Burlington, VT: Hobart J. Shanley and Company, 1905.

Albers, Jan. *Hands on the Land: A History of the Vermont Landscape.* Cambridge, MA: MIT Press, 2000.

Allen, Ira. *The Natural and Political History of the State of Vermont.* 1798. Reprint, Rutland, VT: Charles E. Tuttle Company, 1969.

Andre-Sevigny, P. *Trade and Navigation on the Chambly Canal: A Historical Overview.* Canada: National Historic Parks and Sites Branch, Parks Canada, 1983.

Annesley, William. *A New System of Naval Architecture.* London: W. Nicol. 1822.

Astmann, Stephen K., Ronald F. Kingsley, and Virginia Burleigh LaPointe. "The Burleigh Brothers: Nineteenth Century Titans of the Champlain Basin." *Vermont History* 68 (2000): 185–197.

Aske, Jerry Jr. and Gardiner Lane. *The History of the Shelburne Shipyard and its Shipbuilding Activities During World War II and the Korean Conflict.* Essex Junction, VT: Jerry Aske, Jr. and Gardiner Lane, 1992.

Auld, Joseph. *Picturesque Burlington: A Hand Book of Burlington, Vermont and Lake Champlain.* 2nd ed. Burlington, VT: Free Press Association, 1894.

Bacon, Mayhew Edgar. *The Hudson River From Ocean to Source: Historical—Legendary—Picturesque.* New York: Knickerbocker Press, 1902.

Baker, Charity M., and Douglas S. Fink. *Archaeological Studies of the Main Street Upgrade Project in the City of Burlington, Chittenden County, Vermont, Volume I of II.* Essex Junction, VT: Archaeology Consulting Team, Inc., August 2002.

Barranco, A. Peter Jr., Arthur B. Cohn, Kevin J. Crisman, the late Dennis M. Lewis, and Timothy D. Titus. *Lake Champlain, Lake George, and the Upper Richelieu River Naval and Military Vessel Inventory 1742–1836.* Lake Champlain Maritime Museum, Basin Harbor, VT: August 1999.

Bassett, Seymour T.D. *The Growing Edge: Vermont Villages, 1840–1880.* Montpelier, VT: Vermont Historical Society, 1992.

Bayreuther, William A. III., Kevin J. Crisman, and E. Jan Warren. *A Report on the Nautical Archaeology of Lake Champlain: Results of the 1982 Field Season of the Champlain Maritime Society,* edited by Arthur B. Cohn. Burlington, VT: The Champlain Maritime Society, 1984.

Beach, Allen Penfield. *Lake Champlain as Centuries Pass.* 2nd edition. Basin Harbor, VT: Basin Harbor Club and Lake Champlain Maritime Museum, 1994.

Beers, F.W. *Atlas Map.* Burlington, Chittenden County, 1869. University of Vermont Bailey-Howe Library, Special Collections.

Bellico, Russell P. *Chronicles of Lake George: Journeys in War and Peace.* Fleischmanns, NY: Purple Mountain Press, 1995.

Bellico, Russell P. *Sails and Steam in the Mountains: A Maritime and Military History of Lake George and Lake Champlain.* Fleischmanns, NY: Purple Mountain Press, 1992.

Blow, David J. *Historic Guide to Burlington Neighborhoods.* Burlington, VT: Chittenden County Historical Society, 1991.

Blow, David J. *Historic Guide to Burlington Neighborhoods, Vol. 2.* Burlington, VT: Chittenden County Historical Society, 1997

Blow, David J. "*Vermont I*: Lake Champlain's First Steamboat." *Vermont History* 34 (April 1966), 115–122.

Bourne, Annie Nettleton, trans. *The Voyages and Explorations of Samuel de Champlain, 1604–1616, Narrated by Himself.* Vol. I. New York: Allerton Book Co., 1922.

Bratten, John R. *The Gondola Philadelphia and the Battle of Lake Champlain.* College Station, TX: Texas A&M University Press, 2002.

Buckman, David Lear. *Old Steamboat Days on the Hudson River: Tales and Reminiscences of the Stirring Times that Followed the Introduction of Steam Navigation.* Astoria, NY: J.C. and A.L. Fawcett, Inc., 1990.

Burlington, VT. As a Manufacturing, Business and Commercial Center. Burlington Board of Trade, 1889.

Burlington Daily Free Press. Various issues. Burlington, Vermont. University of Vermont, Bailey-Howe Library, microfilm.

Butler, Benjamin F. *Butler's Book.* Boston, MA: A.M. Thayer & Co., 1892.

Carlisle, Diana L. "Champlain Glass Company: Burlington's First Manufacturing Enterprise." *Vermont History* 68 (2000): 133–162.

Carlough, Peter. *Bygone Burlington.* Burlington, VT: Burlington Bicentennial Committee, 1976.

Carlisle, Lilian Baker. "Background of Burlington's Waterfront Area" and "The Five Old Buildings." *Chittenden County Historical Society Bulletin* 12 (Oct.–Dec. 1977).

Carlisle, Lilian Baker. *Look Around Colchester and Milton, Vermont,* Burlington, VT: Chittenden County Historical Society, 1975.

Carmer, Carl. *The Hudson.* New York: Farrar and Rinehart Inc., 1939.

Chambers, Capt. Wm. *Atlas of Lake Champlain 1779–1780.* Bennington, VT and Montpelier, VT: Vermont Heritage Press and Vermont Historical Society, 1984.

Champlain Transportation Company Files. 9 cartons. University of Vermont, Bailey-Howe Library, Special Collections.

Chase, Jack, Arthur B. Cohn, and Kevin J. Crisman. *A Report on the Nautical Archaeology of Lake Champlain: Results of the 1983 Field Season of the Champlain Maritime Society,* edited by R. M. Fischer. Burlington, VT: Champlain Maritime Society, 1985.

Child, Hamilton. *Gazetteer and Business Directory of Chittenden County, Vermont for 1882–83.* Syracuse, NY: Journal Office, 1882.

Child, Hamilton. *Gazetteer and Business Directory of Washington County, N.Y. for 1871.* Syracuse, NY: Journal Office, 1871.

Chittenden, L.E. *Personal Reminiscences 1840–1890.* New York: Richmond, Croscup, and Co., 1893.

Clifford, George. *Lake Champlain Lighthouses: An Illustrated Guide to the Historic Beacons.* Edited by Lona Helmeci. Plattsburgh, NY: Clinton County Historical Association, 1999.

Cohn, Arthur, and Marshall True. "The Wreck of the *General Butler* and the Mystery of Lake Champlain's Sailing Canal Boats." *Vermont History* 6 (1992)

Cohn, Arthur B. *Phase I Archaeological Assessment for the Proposed Burlington Waterfront Development Project.* Burlington, VT: Champlain Maritime Society, 1984.

Cohn, Arthur B. "The Man and the Boat." *Historic Roots* (May 1995): 10–16.

Cohn, Arthur B. "The Sailing Canal Boats of Lake Champlain." *American Canals* 31 (Spring 2002).

Cohn, Arthur B., Joseph R. Cozzi, Kevin J. Crisman, and Scott A. McLaughlin. *The Archaeological Reconstruction of the Lake Champlain Canal Schooner* General Butler, *Burlington, Chittenden County, Vermont.* Lake Champlain Maritime Museum, Ferrisburgh, VT, 1996.

Cohn, Arthur, B., Joseph R. Cozzi, Kevin J. Crisman, and Scott A. McLaughlin. *Underwater Preserve Feasibility Study of the Lake Champlain Canal Schooner* O.J. Walker, *Burlington, Chittenden County, Vermont.* Ferrisburgh, VT: Lake Champlain Maritime Museum, 1996.

Cook, Flavius J. *Home Sketches of Essex County.* Keeseville, NY: W. Lansing and Son, 1858.

Cozzi, Joseph Robert. *The Lake Champlain Sailing Canal Boat.* Unpublished Ph.D. dissertation. College Station, TX: Texas A&M University, 2000

Crisman, Kevin, *The Eagle: An American Brig on Lake Champlain During the War of 1812.* Shelburne, VT: New England Press; Annapolis, MD: Naval Institute Press, 1987.

Crisman, Kevin J., and Arthur B. Cohn. *When Horses Walked on Water: Horse—Powered Ferries in Nineteenth-Century America.* Washington, DC: Smithsonian Institution Press, 1998.

Crisman, Kevin J., and Arthur B. Cohn. *Lake Champlain Nautical Archaeology since 1980. Journal of Vermont Archaeology,* Vermont Archaeological Society, 1994.

Crockett, Walter Hill. *A History of Lake Champlain: The Record of Three Centuries 1609–1909.* Burlington, VT: Hobart J. Shanley and Co., 1909.

Daniels, Thomas E. *Vermont Indians.* Edited by Kathleen Rowlands. Orwell, VT: Mrs. Thomas Daniels, 1963.

Davis, Dennis J. *The Thames Sailing Barge: Her Gear and Rigging.* Newton Abbot, England: David and Charles; Camden, ME: International Marine Publishing Company, 1970.

Davison, Rebecca, ed. *The* Phoenix *Project: A Report from the Champlain Maritime Society.* Burlington, VT: Champlain Maritime Society, 1981.

Donald, David. *Divided We Fought: A Pictorial History of the War 1861–1865.* WY: Macmillan Company, 1952.

Dunbar, Seymour. *A History of Travel in America.* New York: Tudor Publishing Company, 1937.

Dunnigan, Brian Leigh. *Frontier Metropolis: Picturing Early Detroit 1701–1838.* Detroit, MI: Wayne State University Press, 2001.

Dwight, Timothy. *Travels in New England and New York.* Edited by Barbara Miller Solomon and Patricia M. King. Cambridge, MA: The Belknap Press of Harvard University Press, 1969.

Essex, New York: Lake Champlain's Historic Harbor. Essex Free Library, 1969.

Everest, Allan S. *The War of 1812 in the Champlain Valley.* Syracuse, NY: Syracuse University Press, 1981.

Finch, Roy G. *The Story of the New York State Canals: Historical and Commercial Information.* Albany, NY: J.B. Lyon Company, 1925

Garrity, Richard. *Canal Boatman: My Life on Upstate Waterways.* Syracuse, NY: Syracuse University Press, 1977.

Gekle, William. *A Hudson Riverbook.* Poughkeepsie, NY: Hamilton Reproductions, 1980.

Glenn, Morris F. *The Story of Three Towns: Westport, Essex and Willsboro, New York.* Alexandria, VA: Vanity Press, 1977.

Glenn, Morris F. *Lake Champlain Album, Vol. 2.* Alexandria, VA: Morris Glenn. 1979.

Godfrey, Capt. Fred G. *The Champlain Canal: Mules to Tugboats.* Monroe, NY: LRA Inc., 1994.

Graff, Nancy Price, and E. Thomas Pierce, eds. *Charles Louis Heyde: Nineteenth-Century Vermont Landscape Painter.* Burlington, VT: Robert Hull Fleming Museum, 2001.

Hallie, Bond E. *Boats and Boating in the Adirondacks.* Adirondack Museum: Syracuse University Press, 1995.

Hahn, Thomas S., and Emory L. Kemp. "Canal Terminology of the United States." *Monograph Series 5.* Morgantown, WV. West Virginia University Press, 1998.

Harlow, Alvin F. *When Horses Pulled Boats: A Story of Early Canals.* York, PA: American Canal and Transportation Center, 1983.

Haydon, Roger, ed. *Upstate Travels: British Views of Nineteenth-Century New York.* Syracuse, NY: Syracuse University Press, 1982.

Hemenway, Abby Maria. *Vermont Historical Gazetteer.* Vol.1 (Addison, Bennington, Caledonia, Chittenden and Essex Counties). Burlington, VT, 1867.

Higbee, William Wallace. *Around the Mountains: Historical Essays About Charlotte, Ferrisburgh and Monkton.* Charlotte, VT: Charlotte Historical Society, 1991.

Hill, Ralph Nading. *Lake Champlain: Key to Liberty.* Woodstock, VT: Countryman Press, 1995.

Hill, Henry Wayland. *An Historical Review of Waterways and Canal Construction in New York State.* Buffalo, NY: Buffalo Historical Society, 1908.

Hill, Henry Wayland. *The Champlain Tercentenary; Report of the Champlain Tercentenary Commission.* Albany, NY: J.B. Lyon Co., 1911.

Historical Sketch of Plattsburgh, New York, From its First Settlement to Jan. 1, 1893. Elizabethtown, NY: Crown Point Press, Inc., 1968.

History of Clinton and Franklin Counties, New York. Philadelphia: J.W. Lewis and Co., 1880.

History of Washington Co., New York. 1880. Reprint, Interlaken, NY: Heart of the Lakes Publishing, 1991.

Huden, John comp. *Archaeology in Vermont: Some Reviews Supplemented by Materials from New England and New York.* Rutland, VT: Charles E. Tuttle Company, 1972.

Johnson, Harry, and Frederick S. Lightfoot. *Maritime New York in Nineteenth-Century Photographs.* New York: Dover Publications, Inc., 1980.

Jones, Robert C. "The Early Years, 1830–1886." Vol. 1 of *The Central Vermont Railway: A Yankee Tradition.* Silverton CO: Sundance Books, 1981.

Kalm, Peter. *Travels Into North America.* Translated by John Reinhold Forster. Barre, MA: Imprint Society, 1937.

Kane, Adam I., Sara R. Brigadier, and Christopher R. Sabick. *Lake Champlain Underwater Cultural Resources Survey, Volume VI: 2001 Results, Volume VII: 2002 Results.* Ferrisburgh, VT: Lake Champlain Maritime Museum, 2003.

Kane, Adam I. and Christopher R. Sabick. *Lake Champlain Underwater Cultural Resources Survey, Volume IV: 1999 Results, Volume V: 2000 Results.* Ferrisburgh, VT: Lake Champlain Maritime Museum, 2002.

Keller, Allan. *Life Along the Hudson.* Tarrytown, NY: Sleepy Hollow Press, 1985.

Lake Champlain Tercentenary, July 4-10, 1909. State of New York Education Department, 1909.

Leighton, Marshall O. *Preliminary Report on the Pollution of Lake Champlain*, Washington, DC: Government Printing Office, 1905.

Lossing, Benson J. *The Empire State*. Hartford CT: American Publishing Co., 1888.

Lossing, Benson J. *The Hudson, from the Wilderness to the Sea*. New York: Virtue and Yorston, 1866.

Lundeberg, Philip, K. *The Gunboat* Philadelphia *and the Defense of Lake Champlain in 1776*. Basin Harbor, VT: Lake Champlain Maritime Museum, 1995.

Mackey, Frank. *Steamboat Connections: Montreal to Upper Canada, 1816–1843*. Montreal and Kingston, Canada: McGill-Queen's University Press, 2000.

Manning's Burlington Winooski and Essex Junction Directory 1941–1942, Vol. L11. Springfield, MA: H.A. Manning Company, 1942.

Manning, Gordon P. *Life in the Colchester Reef Lighthouse*. Shelburne, VT: Shelburne Museum, 1988.

McClure, Lois Howe, comp. *Cedar Beach Association, Charlotte, Vermont 1872–1980*.

McKelvey, William J. *Champlain to Chesapeake: A Canal Era Pictorial Cruise*. Berkeley Heights, NJ: Capt. Bill McKelvey, 1978.

McKibben, Alan, and Susan McKibben. *Cruising Guide to the Hudson River, Lake Champlain and the St. Lawrence River: The Waterway from New York City to Montreal and Quebec City*. Burlington, VT: Lake Champlain Publishing Company, 2001.

McKibben, Alan and Douglas Lazarus. *Hudson River Journey: An Artist's Perspective*. Burlington, VT: Lake Champlain Publishing Company, 1999.

Milbert, J. *Itineraire Pittoresque du Fleuve Hudson et Des Parties Laterales*. Paris: 1828–1829. Reprint. Ridgewood, N.J: The Gregg Press, ca. 1970.

Morison, Samuel Eliot. *Samuel de Champlain: Father of New France*. Boston: Little, Brown, and Company, 1972.

Morton, Doris Begor, comp. *Day Before Yesterday*. Whitehall, NY: Town Board of Whitehall, 1977.

Muller, H. N., III. "The Commercial History of the Lake Champlain-Richelieu River Route 1760–1815." Unpublished Ph. D. dissertation. University of Rochester, 1968.

"Nineteenth Annual Report of the City of Burlington, Vermont, for the Year Ending December 31, 1883." Burlington, VT: Free Press Association, 1884.

O Hara, J. E. *Erie's Junior Partner: The Economic and Social Effects of the Champlain Canal Upon the Champlain Valley*. Ann Arbor, MI: University Microfilms International, 1951.

O'Malley, Charles T. *Low Bridges and High Water of the New York State Barge Canal*. Ellenton, FL: Diamond Mohawk Publishing, 1991.

Orr, David Wallis. "The Port of Burlington, Vermont: Site and Situation, A Study in Historical Geography." Unpublished Thesis, University of Vermont, 1972.

Palmer, Peter S. *History of Lake Champlain*. 4th ed. Harrison, NY: Harbor Hill Books, 1983.

Public Documents, Relating to the New-York Canals. New York: William A. Mercein, 1821.

Rann, William S. *History of Chittenden County, Vermont*. Syracuse, NY: D. Mason & Co., 1886.

Rinker, Harry L. "*The Old Raging Erie . . . There Have Been Several Changes*": A Postcard History of the Erie and Other New York State Canals 1895 to 1915. Berkeley Heights, NJ: Canal Captain's Press, 1984.

Rolando, Victor R. *200 Years of Soot and Sweat: The History and Archaeology of Vermont's Iron, Charcoal, and Lime Industries*. Burlington, VT: Vermont Archaeological Society, 1992.

Ross, Ogden. *The Steamboats of Lake Champlain*. Edited by Kevin Graffagnino. Vermont Heritage Press; Lake Champlain Maritime Museum and Lake Champlain Transportation Company, 1997.

Ross, Ogden. *The Steamboats of Lake George 1817 to 1932*. Lake George Steamboat Company, 1932.

Royce, Caroline Halstead. *Bessboro: A History of Westport, Essex Co., N.Y.* Elizabethtown, NY, 1904.

Sanders, Michael S. *The Yard: Building a Destroyer at the Bath Iron Works*. New York: Harper Collins, 1999.

Sabick, Christopher, Anne Lessmann, and Scott McLaughlin. *Lake Champlain Underwater Cultural Resources Survey, Volume II: 1997 Results, Volume III: 1998 Results*. Ferrisburgh, VT: Lake Champlain Maritime Museum, 2000.

Shaw, Ronald E. *Erie Water West: A History of the Erie Canal 1792–1854*. Kentucky: University Press of Kentucky, 1966.

Simpson, Jeffrey. *The Hudson River 1850–1918: A Photographic Portrait*. Tarrytown, NY: Sleepy Hollow Restorations, 1981.

Stratton, Allen L., comp. *History Town of Isle La Motte Vermont: An Account of the Discovery, Settlement, and Interesting and Remarkable Events*. Barre, VT: Northlight Studio Press, 1984.

Strum, Richard M. *Ticonderoga Lake Champlain Steamboat*. Shelburne, VT: Shelburne Museum, 1998.

Sullivan, John L. *A Commentary on the New System of Naval Architecture of William Annesley*. Troy, NY: William Parker. 1823.

U.S. Army Corps of Engineers, New York District. *Recordation of Portions of the Burlington Breakwater in Lake Champlain, City of Burlington, Chittenden County, Vermont in Connection with the Proposed Structural Repair Activities, Final Report*. Panamerican Consultants, Inc., 2001.

Von Susteren, Dick., ed. *A Vermont Century: Photographs and Essays from the Green Mountain State*. Rutland, VT: Rutland Herald, Barre-Montpelier Times Argus, 1999.

The Inland Navigation Surveys of the Western and Northern Inland Lock Navigation Companies 1792. New York: 1992.

Thompson, Zadock. *History of Vermont, Natural, Civil and Statistical*. Burlington, VT: Chauncey Goodrich, 1842.

Twenty-First Annual Report of the City of Burlington, Vermont, for the Year Ending December 31, 1885. Burlington, VT: R.S. Styles, 1886.

Verplanck, William E. And Moses W. Collyer. *The Sloops of the Hudson*. Fleischmanns, NY: Purple Mountain Press, 1984.

Versteeg, Jennie G., ed. *Lake Champlain: Reflections On Our Past*. Burlington, VT: University of Vermont and Vermont Historical Society, 1987.

Visser, Thomas, Elizabeth Rosin, Dr. Peter Thomas, and Prudence Doherty. *Historic Site Review: Burlington Wastewater Treatment Plant Project, Depart of Public Works, Burlington, Vermont*. Burlington, VT: Architectural Conservation and Education Service 1990.

Wallings, H.F. *Map of Chittenden County, Vermont*. Boston & New York: Baker, Tilden & Company, 1857.

Watson, Winslow C. *The Military and Civil History of the County of Essex, New York.* Albany, NY: J. Munsell, 1869.

Weise, Arthur James. *Troy's One Hundred Years: 1789–1889.* Troy, NY: William H. Young, 1891.

Weise, Arthur James. *The History of the City of Albany, New York, from the Discovery of the Great River in 1524, by Verrazzano, to the Present Time.* Albany, NY: E.H. Benner, 1884.

Wilbur, James Benjamin. *Ira Allen: Founder of Vermont 1751–1814.* Boston and New York: Houghton Mifflin Company, 1928.

Wilgus, William J. *The Role of Transportation in the Development of Vermont.* Montpelier, VT: Vermont Historical Society, 1945.

Williams, Earl W. "Champlain Voyage." *Vermont Life* 6 (1952).

Woods, Terry K., comp. *The Ohio and Erie Canal: A Glossary of Terms.* Kent, OH: Kent State University Press, 1995.

On the Champlain Canal, circa 1880.
Courtesy Canal Society of New York State.

Index

J.G. Hindes *at the Otter Creek Basin at Vergennes, Vermont, circa 1890.*
J.G. Hindes was owned by the National Horse Nail Works of Vergennes,
whose owner was Jacob Garus Hindes.
Courtesy the Hindes and Norton Family.

(top)
Bow of Lois McClure, *September 2003.*
Photo by Eric Bessette.

(bottom)
Bluff Bow of an Erie Canal Boat, circa 1900.
Courtesy the Erie Canal Museum.

Boys at Fisk Landing Sitting on the Scow Schooner Wm. Montgomery, *circa 1890.*
Courtesy Vermont Historical Society.

Canal Schooner in North Harbor, the Lake Champlain Maritime Museum Home Port, circa 1896.
Courtesy of the Pratt Family.

Canal Schooner on Otter Creek, circa 1896.
Photo by Charles Parker, courtesy Special Collections, Bailey/Howe Library,
University of Vermont.

Canal Boat Smith M. Weed *Floating with the Current by the Lake Champlain Trans-portation Company Office and their Fleet of Tugboats in Whitehall Harbor, circa 1895.* *Smith M. Weed* was built in 1891 at Champlain, New York by shipwrights Sylvester Alonzo Kellogg and James Averill, Jr. Photograph by artist and writer Howard Pyle.
Courtesy the Fort Ticonderoga Museum.

Canal Boat Family Aboard William J. Higgins *of Ticonderoga at St. John's, Quebec on the Chambly Canal, circa 1910.* American canal boats competed against their Canadian counterparts, such as *Ned of Ottawa*. However, New York State protected the interests of American boatmen by not permitting Canadian vessels to enter the Champlain Canal.
Courtesy the Canal Society of New York State.

Laundry Day Aboard the Canal Boat Bloomingdale *at Whitehall Harbor, circa 1910*. The crews aboard *E.J. Goven* of Schuylerville and *John L. Mock* are preparing for the northbound tow down Lake Champlain. The lake tugs, pictured in the background, left Whitehall for St. John's twice a day with ten to twenty canal boats in single file.
Courtesy the Canal Society of New York State.

Canal Boats Tied Up at a Dock in Jersey City, New Jersey with the New York City Skyline in the Background, circa 1895. Canal boats of various sizes and shapes came to New York harbor from throughout the Northeast, including Virginia, Maryland, Delaware, Pennsylvania, New York, and Vermont.
Photograph by Howard Pyle, courtesy the Fort Ticonderoga Museum.

Back Cover:
Burlington Harbor, circa 1900. In this early twentieth-century photograph, a lone canal schooner can be seen on the right. Although lake shippers tried to remain competitive, transportation by rail, land and air gradually took over.
Courtesy Special Collections, Bailey/Howe Library, University of Vermont.